BOOK OF DAVID
Son of a Kingpin

Written by

DAVID HARRIS JR.
With **THOMAS R. KENNEDY**

EPI Books.

Contact: tomkenpro@gmail.com

Names have been changed to protect those that wish to remain anonymous.

BOOK OF DAVID: Son of a Kingpin.

ACKNOWLEDGMENTS

I'm grateful to all of my dad's friends and family for contributing their heartfelt memories of him – stories that have culminated into this glorious tome.

TABLE OF CONTENTS

FOREWORD

In the corridors of time, where memories intertwine with the whispers of the past, there exists a sacred space within my heart – a place reserved for two extraordinary men who have helped shape my very existence. My brothers, Michael Ray Harris and David Harris, have forever left an irreversible impression upon my soul.

As I embark upon the task of assisting in celebrating David's time on earth with us, I am filled with a bittersweet mix of love, admiration, and profound loss. But I draw from the strength that lives in me from living in the same household with such loving and strong men.

David's story cannot be properly told without understanding that David's tenacity was influenced by Michael's never-quit attitude. He was inseparable from his older brother, Michael. Michael was a father figure for us both, always concerned with the well-being of his immediate as well as extended family. Michael, or as the world would come to know him, Harry O, is also a visionary, a born leader – an enigmatic force of nature who breathed life into Death Row Records, forever changing the landscape of the music industry. His creative genius and unyielding determination transformed the rap genre, propelling it to unimaginable heights.

Through orchestrating the music that Death Row produced, Harry O became a voice for the voiceless, a beacon of hope for those trapped within the confines of a harsh reality. His visionary prowess painted vivid pictures, shedding light on the struggles, triumphs, and injustices of our time. His creative brilliance and unwavering passion remain a source of inspiration, forever etched into the annals of music history. The legacy he created with Death Row Records continues to reverberate through the halls of music history, and the world will forever celebrate him as a true hip hop pioneer.

This unyielding spirit, a flame that refused to be extinguished, was instilled in David and I. And though his journey was fraught with tribulations, his conviction remained unbreakable. Michael's tale is far from being finished as he continues to guide those that he love through the rhythms of life.

As I reflect upon our shared experiences, I am reminded of the countless moments where Michael's unwavering support lifted all of us from the depths of despair, his infectious laughter filling the room, breathing life into our shared dreams and aspirations.

And then there was David, compassionately called Black Dave, my beloved brother – a black God, as I fondly remember him. A bigger than life figure that would change his small section of the world without that ever being his ultimate goal. He was just sharing a tiny slice of his love, a love that taught many how to truly love – unconditional love, unmatched by any.

He possessed an insatiable thirst for life, a hunger for adventure that knew no bounds. David's spirit was as untamed as the wind, and his love for speed was a testament to his fearless nature. Every moment spent in his company was filled with boundless energy and an undeniable zest for life.

Whether it was the thrill of dashing down the highway in one of his exotic cars, the rush of soaring through the sky on a speedboat, or simply basking in the radiance of a lovely day, David's infectious enthusiasm left an everlasting impression on all who had the privilege of crossing his path.

But life, as we are often reminded, is a delicate fabric – woven with joy, sorrow, and the unexpected twists of fate. It was in one such tragic twist that David's journey was cut short, leaving a void in my heart that can never be filled. The pain of losing him reverberates through my very being, a constant reminder of life's fragility and the momentary nature of our existence. Yet, in the midst of my grief, I find solace in the knowledge that David's spirit lives on, forever etched into the hearts of those who were fortunate enough to share in his magnificent presence.

For David, life was a symphony in motion – a kaleidoscope of exhilaration and passion. And if he had the power to choose his own path to eternity, I am certain he would have opted for a fate intertwined with the thrill of speed. It was in those moments, with the wind in his hair and his heart pounding with excitement, that David truly came alive. And though his physical form may no longer grace this earth, the essence of his being continues to inspire and ignite the spirits of all who carry a piece of Black Dave within them.

As I delve into the depths of his story, I am acutely aware of the responsibility bestowed upon me to capture the essence of this remarkable man. This foreword serves as a mere glimpse into his extraordinary life – a life, although short-lived but filled with love, passion, resilience, and the unyielding pursuit of dreams. It is a testament to the power of brotherhood, the bonds that transcend time and space, and the profound impact that one's presence can have on the lives of others.

In these pages, you will find not only the tales of David but also the story of an enduring sisterhood – a testament to the unbreakable bond that love forges. It is a journey through the triumphs and tribulations, the laughter and tears, and the relentless pursuit of greatness. It is a celebration of a soul who dared to dream, who dared to challenge the status quo, and who dared to leave an impressive mark upon the world.

As you immerse yourself in the chapters that follow, I invite you to embark on a voyage – a voyage that will transport you through the heights of extreme brilliance, the depths of human resilience, and the timeless essence of love. Within these pages, you will witness the triumph of the human spirit, the birth of an Angel, and the heartbreaking tragedy of his life cut short.

It is my sincerest hope that David's story will ignite a flame within you – a flame that will inspire you to pursue your dreams with unwavering determination, to cherish the bonds of family and friendship, and to honor the memories of those who have shaped your own personal journey.

To David Harris, my black God, your zest for life and love of speed continue to reverberate through our souls. Your presence lingers in the wind, whispering tales of adventure and reminding us to embrace each moment with unbridled joy.

And to all who have been touched by the lives of this extraordinary man, carry his legacy with you, for he serves as a reminder that within each of us lies the power to shape our own destinies, to leave your own fingerprint upon the earth, and to live a life that defies the boundaries of time.

With love, admiration, and an unwavering commitment to preserving your story, Starlisa Young.

THE BEGINNING

Fannie Jordan, my paternal grandmother, affectionately called Mamo (pronounced Ma'am mo) by her grandchildren, arrived in Los Angeles in the 1950's from Oak Grove, a tiny town in northeast Louisiana, twenty minutes from the Arkansas border, in the middle of nowhere. Fannie came to LA with aspirations to make a different life for herself than just slaving in the sweltering heat on someone's farm or being a maid in some white person's house. And she was sick of having to enter through the back door to have a meal at a restaurant.

In the bright lights of LA, her dreams of a wonderful future began to unfold as she secured gainful employment as a waitress, making more money in a day than she could make in a week in Oak Grove. Eventually, she would have two sons, her firstborn, Michael and her second son, David, with a man not totally invested in family, leaving her and their two sons to fend for themselves.

Fannie was determined to give her sons, more than life had given her, and she would often work multiple jobs to keep a roof over their heads and food on the table. She learned that people liked her wholesome personality and genuine conversation – qualities that helped her thrive as a waitress.

As much as she loved her boys, Fannie realized that they needed to experience a different world, a world that would shape their understanding of life and challenge their perspectives.

During their pre-teen years, she decided to send them to her mother, Big Mama, as she was called by family members and people that loved her. Big Mama lived in Terry, Louisiana, a small, tight-knit community nestled among the sprawling fields of the South. It was a tiny town in West Carrol Parish, a few miles north of the small two-stop-light town of Oak Grove.

Fannie knew that her sons would encounter a vastly different environment from the bustling streets of Los Angeles. She hoped that by spending their summers with her mother, Michael and David would gain a deeper appreciation for their roots as well as develop a broader understanding of life.

On the day of their departure, they walked into the Greyhound bus station, downtown Los Angeles on 6th and Los Angeles Street. The intercom system crackled to life and the PA announcer said, "Buses are loading now, for Las Vegas, Nevada, Denver, Colorado and Dallas, Texas.

The three of them found the location of the Dallas bus, the bus that they would ride upon until they reached Dallas, where they would transfer to the Louisiana bus. The boys kissed their mother, excitement and nervousness danced in Michael and David's eyes as the two boys climbed aboard the bus. They hurried to their seats, finding their mother's concerned eyes as they waved from the window.

The bus lurched forward, commencing their adventure. A few miles into the ride, the rhythmic clatter of the wheels against the asphalt street lulled them into a peaceful slumber.

The boys would wake to witness for the first time, miles of open highway, an armadillo along the road-side and a coyote in the distance. And the boys witnessed interesting character traits in people. A strange looking man even tried to sell them a joint. Two days later, they reached

Dallas Texas. Michael followed his mother's instructions and they transferred to a bus headed to all points in Louisiana, including the small town of Oak Grove.

The next morning, they arrived at a tiny outpost that was an extension of a cafe. The boys were greeted by the warm embrace of Big Mama. Love radiated from her like the shining sun on a magnificent summer's day.

They loaded their luggage into her car and off they went toward what would become their summer vacation home. The boys would learn that the locals called where Big Mama lived, "the sticks."

The boys would see animals and reptiles that they had never seen: chickens, pigs, black Crowes, lizards and occasionally a snake. At night, fireflies would light up the dark sky. David would catch a few fireflies, placing them in a jar to watch their lights blink on and off well into the night.

The summer corduroys, matching button-down shirts and loafers that Fannie had (the boys first fashion expert) coordinated, made it obvious to anyone that saw the boys that they were not from those parts.

Big Mama enveloped them in a world steeped in Southern hospitality and traditions. But their home away from home would severely test their understanding of equality and justice.

As the boys settled into their new routine, they quickly realized that Oak Grove held a different set of rules and expectations for black people. They witnessed firsthand the unsettling reality of racial segregation – a system that sought to divide people based on the color of their skin. In this small Southern town, white men still clung to the misguided belief that they were inherently superior to their Black counterparts.

Michael and David's eyes were opened to the stark contrast between the segregated South and the more progressive attitudes of their home town. They learned that even stepping foot in certain establishments required them to enter through the back door, a silent reminder of their perceived place in society.

Big Mama, a wise and resilient woman, understood the importance of discussing these issues with her grandsons. She spent hours recounting stories of her own ugly experiences, emphasizing the strength and perseverance of black people. She taught them that love and understanding were the most potent weapons against ignorance and injustice.

Big Mama taught them ways to challenge the backward thinking that persisted in Oak Grove and throughout the south, and the number one rule was to stay clear of white women.

Big Mama would cook a delectable meal every night, and during supper the three of them would engage in thought-provoking conversations about racial prejudice and the importance of standing up for what was right. These in-depth conversations caused the boy's horizons to expand and the development of a deep empathy for the struggles faced by the black community in the south.

Throughout the summers spent in Oak Grove, Michael and David witnessed both the beauty and the ugliness of the South. They saw the lush green landscapes and experienced the warm hospitality that defined Southern culture but yet were confronted with the harsh and ugly realities of racism. These contrasting experiences helped shape their understanding of the world, instilling within them a determination to take on the struggle with only the attitude of winning.

As that first summer drew to a close, Michael and David returned to Los Angeles with enlightened minds. They carried with them the memories of their time spent with Big Mama and their family in Louisiana, along with a newfound sense of purpose.

Fannie embraced her sons tightly as they stepped off the bus, she saw in their eyes that their journey had transformed them. And a surge of pride washed over her. As Fannie had hoped, it was obvious that Big Mama's teachings and the experiences in Oak Grove had helped to shape their identities.

On the ride back to their house, Fannie glanced at her sons with proud eyes, knowing that her decision to send them to Oak Grove had been a turning point in their lives. Over the passing days, she noticed that they took care of their chores without her having to remind them and smiled within. She knew from growing up with her mother that her stern tutelage had sunk deeply into her boys, providing them with a Louisiana backbone, which would give them a toughness not known by kids in Los Angeles.

She noticed how mature they now sounded. And she knew that through their experiences, Michael and David had come to appreciate life on a completely different level, a level where it was clearly understood that a good life only came through hard work. Fannie understood that ignorance and prejudice had a way of leaving a bad taste in the mouth of the insulted person, and she knew that their worldview had been forever changed. She was glad for the experiences they had gained, teaching them the importance of standing up for themselves, even in the face of a fierce adversary.

As Michael grew older, he began to help out any way that he could, taking odd and end jobs. A faithful eldest son, eager to help ease his mother's struggles. He blazed a trail that was so bright that it was impossible for David not to recognize it. David following in his older brother's footsteps, pitched in and did his part. Soon the dynamic duo made life easier for their mother.

By the time, the boys became young adults, they saw the vast opportunity that presented itself in the hair industry. Young black men and women had found a new hair style to wear called Jerry Curls. This Jerry Curl process would soften and create larger curls in naturally curly black hair.

Michael found a school, Cindy Lu's in Leimert Park, to teach him. And David was right on his heels. At the school, David would discover that he was a hit with young ladies and his charm blossomed. Some women thought of David as being very handsome, handsome enough to become a movie star and encouraged him to go into acting.

The brothers began making money doing hair, right as rock cocaine was introduced into the black communities of LA, and the young men fell in line with this venture. They had enough money to purchase a small amount of cocaine to sell.

With Michael's brilliant business mind and David's charisma, the brothers' illegal drug operation would soar well passed many of their peers, earning them the right to escape poverty. And soon the men were wearing fancier clothes, driving exotic cars, and living in upscale areas of the city. The brothers, knowing that selling drugs couldn't last without them getting locked up or killed, would open businesses to convert their illegal gains.

While Michael was the serious businessman type. David was carefree, just wanting to be rich. Michael would open all sorts of businesses from limousine companies to rental car agencies. And Dave would follow his big brother's lead.

Along the way, David discovered that he was an excellent salesman, his sells methods so compelling that they should have been taught in Universities. His technique was filled with grace, ease and flow, never leaving his customer feeling like something was being forced upon him or her. As the saying goes, he could sell snow to an Eskimo. With a big smile and a loving heart, many people that he met, instantly fell in love. Soon, his was a household name in the underworld.

Mike set his sights on the burgeoning world of Hip-Hop and made plans to open his own record company. As fate would have it, Mike didn't escape the long arm of the law. But with the plans already in motion in his mind, from a dreaded prison cell, Mike opened Death Row Records, the company that created the likes of Dr. Dre, Snoop Dog, and the much beloved Tupac.

THE SECOND SON

David Harris Sr. would meet Robin Melton along his travels. And the two of them would engage in a romance that produced me, David Harris Jr., the eldest of two children from this union. My father had a son from a previous relationship, Davon Harris, making me his second son, same as my dad.

I mostly know my dad through friends that knew and loved him, many of which speak highly of his ability to be a compassionate man in a world ruled by violent chaos. As I hear their voices recalling their loving memories of him singing in my mind, I can almost see his long gait and loving smile as he strides toward me.

I don't think there has been enough studies done on what happens to the mind of children from a fatherless home. How a young male child, having just one parent, a mother, can change their life's trajectory because the normal course of growth is interfered with when there is no advice of how to be a man from a man that one can trust.

I was two years old when my dad tragically lost his life in a boating accident. My mom was seven months pregnant with my brother, Donovan Michael Harris. I didn't know why things seemed so out of place nor could describe what I was feeling. But not having my father in our home left me feeling inadequate, angry, sad, and frustrated – left me to battle a rollercoaster of emotions. A rollercoaster that I occasionally ride on till this day.

I was force fed the heartbreak story early. As soon as I was old enough to understand what mom was telling me about my biological father's absence and that he would not ever be there, it felt like the universe had cheated me. Anger, sadness, frustration, and inadequacy would follow me throughout my young years, affecting my actions and many of my decisions.

From the time I bumped my head on Aunt Star's coffee table, causing it to bleed, her bandage on my wound momentarily stopping the bleeding, but as she rushed me to the hospital, the whole ride, I was crying inconsolably for my father. It just felt like he should be there. I desperately wanted him to be there.

I just felt like if he was there everything would be better. When I had my first violent encounter and realized that my father hadn't shown me how to fight, I once again felt cheated. Each of those times and many more, I felt the intensity of his loss.

The knowledge that my hero had fallen became a moment of clarity – my first taste of how unfair life could be. This feeling of loss lingered for years in my heart and mind, essentially becoming a fact that I built my foundation upon.

Every new venture I entered into would cause a "what if" to surface in my mind. I started my first business and felt as though I needed dad's help to architect a winning business concept. When I saw my friends with their fathers, I felt happy that they had a father but I couldn't help but feel cheated, their good fortune being evidence of what could've been.

When I saw Uncle Deucy and my Godfather Terry with their kids, although they were family, I was left with a bittersweet feeling. But I loved seeing the impactful value both of those men brought into their children's life.

In their relationships with their children, I could picture what it would've been like with my dad and that picture was one of the most beautiful masterpieces that my eyes have ever beheld, causing me to yearn more for a father-son duo.

My cousins La Rue and Unique became close confidants because they also suffered the same circumstances of not having a father in the home. LaRue's father was murdered by a drug dealer rival, and gang violence claimed the life of Unique's father. The connection to their stories forever held a place in my heart, our bond, the reality of our fatherless struggle.

I was fortunate to have several surrogate fathers: my uncles, Michael, Deucy and Terry. As I got older, Deucy came around less and less due to his busy lifestyle. Terry, whom I called Uncle TC, was always there for birthdays, graduations, and my oldest son's birth.

Uncle TC was actually my godfather and he became a great example of a friend. He really made me feel like a part of his family. He made sure I knew that I came from a different type of bloodline – one of respectful hustlers, entrepreneurs and businessmen. "We are Street Royalty," Uncle Terry would say.

For a few years during my adolescence, mom was with Anthony Chambers. When he became the man of the house, he played a pivotal role in my life as a father figure and mentor.

He's my youngest brother, Anthony's dad. I remember that he was a smooth guy that stayed dressedup. Every so often, he would pick me up from school and I loved when he did because we went straight from school to Toys-R-Us. I could pickany toy that I wanted, then he would take me to get a burger, pizza or whatever my little heart desired. Of course, he quickly soared to the topof my favorites list, if not my all-time favorite. And I began calling him Big Ant.

When Big Ant found out I was selling drugs in the 8th grade, he issued a stern warning to stop immediately, reminding me that my actions would provide me the opportunity to be in a bunk next to my uncle. I appreciate his concern till this day and that he cared enough to be a voice of reason in my life. Big Ant had warned me as I imagined a father would and it felt right. Direction from a male point of view was refreshing. Unfortunately, he wasn't around long enough for his lessons to firmly take hold in my young mind.

During my teen years, in moments of doubt and uncertainty, I would look to the heavens and find comfort in the thought that dad was watching over me, cheering me on. It was as if his larger than life personalities had transcended the bounds of mortality, his spirit forever intertwining with mine.

Even with all the guidance I was receiving and the thoughts of my father watching over me, the streets would still claim me. During the race riots in Los Angeles, I enlisted in a gang. My fourteen-year-old mind felt that I needed the support of others against those that were lining up against us, whom we code named, the enemy.

By the time that I became aware that I was an independent thinker, the streets had taught me how to hustle. Mom had always told me that dad was a businessman owning exotic car lots, among other prosperous businesses. And I desired to bring my family back to that type of prominence.

We all give ourselves a reason to be whoever we become. I was committing senseless crimes for cash or what I thought was respect. Without ever knowing my father was a kingpin, I traveled down the same road, more from necessity to put food in my stomach than wanting to be a participant in the illicit drug trade.

But the drug dealing made me a local celebrity, which I loved and even later craved. My shop was set up across the street from California State University Northridge (CSUN). The college clientele loved my rambunctious sixteen-year old attitude. In a short time, I was a teen living like a young kingpin. And when I tell you that college kids party hard, it doesn't even begin to express their intensity. They're animals!

I started having issues with my mother's apartment management. He felt that my business stopped his college tenants from paying rent because they spent all their money on drugs. He confronted me and while he was exhibiting an aggressive posture, I wasn't worried at all. At six feet, a hundred and eighty pounds, I could handle myself well. When he realized he wasn't going to intimidate me with his words, he had the audacity to spit in my face. And I instantly commenced to whipping his ass. I thought he had taken his ass whipping like a man as he limped away to lick his wounds. But the next day, a process server knocked on our door with a three notice to leave his property, and he had also filed a restraining order against me.

My mother wasn't ready for another move, so she stayed put. But her mother, who we affectionately call Maa-Maa, supported the actions of me defending myself against an adult male. Of course, I hadn't told her the real reason for our confrontation.

Maa-Maa didn't agree with me moving by myself, so she picked up and moved across the street with me. The new apartment was even closer to the college, and again business began to boom!

I had more clients as well as more freedom. Mom not being around all the time allowed me to spread my wings. In a few months, I was living a college rock star life. From my "college trap house," I made thousands in a very short period of time.

While I was still in middle school, on numerous occasions, teachers had tried to snitch on me but my mother and grandmother didn't believe them. On one occasion, my class went on a field trip that I didn't attend. And some kids got busted with weed, they immediately pointed their fingers at me. The school didn't expel them but they did expel me. My mother and grandmother didn't believe the boy they had raised could be involved in such shenanigans.

It wasn't until one day, Maa-Maa came home early from work and caught me slipping. The scale I used to weigh product and a few ounces were left out on our Ottoman. My run had lasted for years but now my little secret was exposed.

Although, my grandmother had always been very supportive of my desires, the drug dealing was the last straw. She was a Seventh Day Adventist and opposed everything about drug dealing and the world that surrounded the Devil's work.

Maa-Maa sit me down and expressed how she strongly disagreed with the direction my life was heading. And my love for her made me consider the damage I was doing to those that loved me. And I decided to step back from that lifestyle.

When I shut down my operations, I became desperate, not having the money I had grown accustomed to, and decided to start doing home invasions. I robbed one of my best clients without knowing it was his house, which blew up in my face.

Once my mother and grandmother learned of my criminal activity, the end of me living with either of them was imminent. Drug dealing, home invasion and assault had quickly shaped the ugly person I had become.

One day, I left the apartment to stash my guns and drugs, and upon my returned I was standing in fresh sawdust from the locks on the apartment being changed. Another lesson taught. I now had restraining orders at my mother's and grandmother's, and left on the streets. From the things I had been taught from a young child, homelessness wasn't a viable option, so I stepped up my hustling game, selling drugs to any willing client.

Some of the greatest highlights of my young adult years, was when my Uncle Michael would call from prison, and around this time, he was calling frequently. I remember once while I was just a struggling college student, and down to my last three hundred dollars, I inquired what I should do to make it double. He knew exactly what to do, and it wasn't what I expected. He laid out a plan in broad strokes of how I should sell T-shirts.

I had been thinking about selling T-shirts at college with popular rap lyrics on them, and my uncle gave me the name "Hip-Hop Quotables, and my business was launched. On my first shirts, I printed the phrase, "Everyday I'm Hustlin'" and those shirts sold out immediately.

After the success of our first venture, it seemed like he and I was scheming something on every call. As my uncle's deep bass voice rumbled through the phone line, I clung to every word. On some of our fifteen-minute conversations, we would discuss rebuilding the Harris Brand as he instituted his business philosophy into my psyche. Those deep conversations were the source of big dreams for me. I didn't know it at that moment but this was the inception of my becoming a businessman.

Although, I was being tutored on how to become a successful businessman, bills still had to be paid, so I was juggling. A few years later, at the tender age of twenty-one, I was living in a 2.2 million-dollar home in Porter Ranch, an upscale area in the San Fernando Valley section of Los Angeles. But I was smart enough to know that selling drugs wasn't a sustainable business model, so I kept learning all I could about the record business, hoping to one day have the same success as I had found in selling drugs.

Every day, I would look forward to Uncle Mike's phone call. They were refreshing moments for me. On many days, he and I would discuss a variety of topics, the family, women, and my father's ability to maneuver difficulty better than all others. He shared with me what he was learning about being a responsible person as he was examining and understanding those theories for himself.

Uncle Michael helped me to believe in myself, us, and the mission ahead. Those conversations begin to ease the heartbreak of the loss of my father. My uncle made me feel like his son. I will be forever grateful that he gave me hope when I needed it most.

Through him, I discovered my love for entertainment and the significance of my last name. Bringing my family back to prominence through entertainment became my goal. Uncle Mike, the architect of Death Row Records, was more than an adequate mentor.

Right around this time, Big Ant had become a record executive, and he was very instrumental in helping me to get my first major deal signed, a collaboration with an artist called Mike Free.

During this same time period, I became acutely aware that something was awry with the handling of my uncle's company. Voices began to say ludicrous things about the man that had the heart and guts to invest in a fellow that he had never met, plus tutor him on how to become a successful CEO.

It was disheartening to witness the power struggle between the man that was given a chance to run the company and my uncle that gave him that chance. It seemed so ridiculous. How could he turn his back on someone that had made him, an unknown figure, relevant?

On so many nights, I hated that the controversy surrounding Death Row kept my family from enjoying the deserving proceeds from the company my uncle founded. The wounds inflicted were slow to heal. Here we were, hood royalty, and struggling to keep the ship afloat, while some joker was enjoying the proceeds of an invention he didn't invent. I often wondered when Karma would launch its attack.

But Uncle Mike was calm during this whole process. I couldn't even imagine being in such a desperate situation, trapped in prison while dealing with the dilemma of fighting for a company I founded. It never felt like my uncle let the frustration overwhelm him as we discussed a way forward.

What I had hoped for with my father, my uncle was providing. These were some of the happiest and proudest moments of my existence. I opened up completely to learn all that he was teaching me. Along with my tutor teaching me all that he knew about the record industry, my search to know more about my dad led me to those who knew him best, and the combination of both helped me to grow into a different type of person.

My pursuit to learn about the record business didn't come easy but I was determined to understand it all. And my uncle was patient, lacing me with the intricacies of the business and how to be a productive CEO.

During this very enlightening period, my precious Aunt Traci was diagnosed with cancer, a drastic turning point in my life. The pressure of it all was almost unbearable. As she lived out her final moments in a home hospice, I desperately wished I had the money to change her conditions, to change all of our conditions.

As I wrestled with the idea of being able to spend more time with her before she was no longer with us, I realized how proud my aunt would be of me making something of myself, and I dove deeply into the music business, vowing to make it work. I was determined to be the best version of myself, a man that my family could be proud of. I diligently studied everything about the business that I could get my hands on, and I listened intently on every phone call with Uncle Michael, driven by the determination to be the difference maker in our family.

And during this process, it started to become clearer. And I either found or created the solutions I sought. As my business acumen increased, I decided to open Blank Kanvaz, my own entertainment company.

Being named after such a dynamic man, I knew that I had big shoes to fill. Now, armed with an entertainment company, my life-long dream of bringing dad's story to life, could be fulfilled.

The boating accident claimed his life at twenty-six years old – much too early and the world needed to know about this dynamic personality that graced this earth with his loving and charming personality, albeit for a short time. But the lives he touched would forever carry the lessons learned from this compassionate being.

And although, an accident is how some reported the story, I would later learn that my dad could swim. So, the question remains how could he have drowned?

As I met more and more people that knew him, I felt the genuineness in their words as they expressed their love for my father. One man said that there was no one in the world that could have a bad thing to say about David Harris. And I was drawn to know more.

My search would lead me to all corners of LA, from the bottoms where dad grew up, which is from Figueroa to Alameda and from Slauson to the edge of downtown, to all other black and brown communities in LA, all the way to Watts, as well as Compton and Long Beach.

I would began to learn interesting aspects about the development of the men that were bold enough to defy all odds, even bold enough to challenge the government. Men that movies would be made about their lives. Many of them were born during an era when mothers were rewarded with government assistance, i.e., a bi-weekly welfare check (the first and the fifteen) for not having a father in the home. Uncle Sam had vowed to take care of the black woman while black men were being systematically castrated – stripped away from jobs to provide for their family, stripped away from raising their children, some of these men turned to drugs and alcohol, themselves becoming dependent on the government for assistance. These studies were conducted during the Reconstruction Era, and the perpetrators of this new evil called "Welfare" would keep the black family unit dysfunctional.

Then young black men rose up all over this country that wouldn't dare take a hand-out from the government. Their objective was to become as rich as their white counterparts. And they would find ways to make money and take care of their family by any means necessary.

Many of the men that knew dad recounted that during the 1980s in the gritty underworld of Los Angeles, emerged a figure known as David "Black Dave" Harris. This era marked a time where power was measured by fear and respect. From the outside, he appeared to be just another player in the risky game of crime and illicit activities, but those who knew him understood that he possessed a unique skill set – one that went far beyond his reputation as a streetwise hustler.

Black Dave had a gift – a talent for negotiation that surpassed that of even the most seasoned diplomats. He had an innate ability to diffuse conflicts and find peaceful resolutions in the most volatile situations. His words carried weight and influence, and even the most hardened criminals would hesitate to cross him.

Genetics are amazing. That same trait, I also possess. And even before I ever understood exactly how to utilize it properly, I was intervening in conflicts and defusing them. As I became more knowledgeable, this ability was a valuable tool.

While others in the underworld reveled in violence, Black Dave saw the bigger picture. He recognized that war slowed down profits and left a trail of destruction in its wake that police forces could easily follow. He understood that finding a better solution, one that avoided bloodshed and preserved the status quo, was not only morally sound but also financially advantageous.

The conflicts that were arising during this time, started with small disputes – territorial battles, disagreements over drug distribution, and personal vendettas. Black Dave would step in, his imposing presence commanding attention. He had a way of making everyone involved feel heard and understood. He would listen intently, absorbing the grievances and frustrations of both sides, and then with calm and calculated words, he would present an alternative path.

His negotiation skills were unmatched. He would find common ground, areas of compromise that both parties could agree upon. It wasn't about winning or losing; it was about finding a resolution that benefited everyone involved. Black Dave had an uncanny ability to see the bigger picture, to understand the long-term consequences of violence and conflict.

Word of Black Dave's diplomatic prowess spread like wildfire throughout the criminal underworld. His reputation grew, and soon, his mere presence could de-escalate a tense situation. Rival gang leaders and drug lords would seek his counsel and intervention when conflicts arose.

But for all his success in conflict resolution, Black Dave remained oblivious to the impact he was having on the streets of Los Angeles. He saw his actions as a means to an end, driven primarily by his desire to maintain a stable and profitable criminal empire. He didn't recognize the power he held, the potential to bring about positive change in a world tainted by violence and chaos.

In communities were black male masculinity was finding its Alpha, finding a big brother or father figure, to get what they couldn't get in their mother-only homes, all sorts of tragedies were occurring. Many young black men's lives were slain on the streets of Los Angeles or locked behind prison bars. Much of the advice these young men were receiving was that of a guy with a gang mentality, a mentality that was spreading across the landscape. Sometimes this guy was only slightly older than the inquirer but his decision to accept the gang's calling first, earned him the right to be called Big Homie. And that title carried respect amongst their ranks.

Whether by design or pure luck, possibly a combination of both, Dave left these types of mindsets curious. And with as much money as he had, many of them didn't know if he would send someone to avenge any disrespect toward him, so they were left spellbound. Not knowing what to think about this revered figure, their indecisiveness left Black Dave safe.

As the years passed, Dave's influence continued to grow. He became a distinguished figure, sought after not only for his criminal expertise but also for his wisdom and guidance. All those that didn't love him, respected him. Underneath his handsome exterior, he possessed a sharp intellect and a deep understanding of human nature. His negotiation skills were honed to perfection, and his words carried the weight of authority.

Though Black Dave may not have recognized the true extent of his impact, his legacy was undeniable. He had shown that peace and prosperity could be achieved even in the darkest corners of society. His actions saved countless lives, prevented countless conflicts, and ensured that the wheels of illicit commerce continued to turn.

In the eyes of many, Black Dave became more than just a criminal mastermind – he became a symbol of honor and a voice of reason in a dark and unforgiving world. His ability to handle situations with finesse and tact earned him the respect of both his allies and adversaries alike. In the shadows of Los Angeles, Black Dave's name became synonymous with diplomacy – a testament to the power of a humble soul.

Eulogies this extensive are usually reserved for famous people. Award-winning prose are spoken about them posthumously. But rarely, if ever, do you get to hear on this level how friends and family felt about a person from an everyday walk of life, especially how they truly felt about a major figure from the underworld.

Sure, we've seen movies like The Godfather and American Gangster. But these contributions are usually soiled and sullied in the commentary of how vicious the men were that engaged in this illicit activity to get what they desired – murder usually being the main plot-line of these stories.

I have met with all sorts of people during my search. Many of which are now my uncles. And what I learned most from them all, was my dad, David "Black Dave" Harris was a well-loved man. Boss Hustla, a movie about his life is in pre-production.

I want to honor his memory by embodying the same fearlessness and passion for life that he exemplified. As I pilot my own journey through life, I carry his legacy with me as a guiding light. I often wonder what advice he would have given me, what words of wisdom he would have shared. In those moments of contemplation, I can almost hear his voice, encouraging me to chase my dreams, to embrace the unknown, and to never settle for mediocrity.

His tragic passing serves as a constant reminder of how momentary life can be, and the importance of seizing every opportunity. As a result of my extensive research, I've learned the importance of cherishing the connections we forge along life's unpredictable path. And I am determined to make the most of my own existence, to pursue my passions with unwavering dedication, and to live a life that would make dad proud.

A FATHER'S IMPACT

Receiving guidance from uncles only once in a while wasn't sufficient enough to help complete me as a person. They all had their own children, and of course their children were their first priority, which made their guidance for me inconsistent.

One of my father's friends told me that no one in my dad's whole crew planned to have their children follow their footsteps into a life of crime. They all wanted the greatest education for their children, sending them to the best private schools in the city. This made me think, "What if my father had been here? Could I have avoided all of my delinquent choices? Would my childhood been totally different?"

At the birth of my first child, I decided to make him proud of having a father constantly in his life. I vowed to give him a different upbringing from the one that I had experience. I was, and still determined to be a father that is fully dedicated that leads by example. I think the combination of my upbringing and my vow helped me make better choices in regards to my children.

To fulfill my promise, I created a list of three goals to accomplish:

1. **Alive and Healthy:** If God is willing and I am alive, I will stay as healthy as possible so I can do all sorts of activities with my children.

2. **Teach my Experiences:** I've put a positive spin on anything negative in my upbringing, turning it into lessons that I've incorporated

into my parenting.

3. **Befriend my Child:** When my child was old enough to make decisions (around five years old) I asked him did he love me. Once we established that he did, I asked him did he want to enter into a partnership with me. If he said, no, end of discussion. But if I got a yes, then I would seek his agreement in allowing me to be the senior partner, explaining that since I had lived on the earth longer, I had a little more experience. But I would also add, that I would only be the senior partner until such time as he was old enough to become my equal partner. After his agreement was confirmed, if there was ever a situation that arose that required discipline, I would instruct him on the proper way as I would a business partner. If I sensed any resistance, I simply reminded him of my status in our relationship that he had agreed to.

I have four boys, so now we're a major corporation. Staying on course to complete these goals added tremendous purpose to my life. It became my Ultimate Challenge.

Growing up without a father was an incredibly difficult experience, both emotionally and physically. The absence of a male role model left a significant void in my life, particularly when it came to learning and understanding what it meant to not just be a man, but how to be a productive businessman and leader.

While my mother may have been a source of love and support, there were certain aspects of masculinity that could only be learned from a male figure such as being a protector and provider. Learning how to provide and protect a family are two of the most important roles of a patriarch. So, to say I was unequipped being raised in a single-mother household is grossly understated. I had to find ways to develop a sense of masculinity despite the absence of a father.

The Importance of Male Influence

Having a male influence during childhood is crucial for the development of young boys. Fathers often serve as mentors, teaching important life skills, and providing guidance on how to handle life from a man's perspective. Without this influence, boys may feel lost or unsure about their identity and place in society. The absence of a father figure can lead to a lack of understanding of how to behave, communicate, and interact with others in a masculine way.

Seeking Role Models

One way to address the absence of a father figure is to actively seek out positive male role models in your life. This could be an uncle, grandfather, teacher, coach, family friend, or an in-law. Male guidance doesn't stop when the boy comes of age. I still seek male guidance in the continual journey of bettering myself.

You should look for individuals who embody the qualities you admire and respect in a man. They can provide valuable guidance and serve as a source of inspiration and support. Building relationships with these role models can help fill the void left by the absence of a father.

Exploring Male Bonding Activities

Growing up, there may be a longing to engage in traditionally masculine activities such as playing catch, learning to shoot hoops, dealing with the opposite sex, participating in outdoor adventures, as well as financial literacy/leadership. While it may not be the same as having a father to teach you these skills, seek out opportunities to engage in these activities with friends or mentors. Join a sports team, participate in community programs, or explore hobbies that align with your interests. Not only will this help you develop new skills, but it will also provide an opportunity to bond with other males and learn from their experiences.

Building Emotional Resilience

One aspect of masculinity that often goes unaddressed is emotional resilience. Society often expects men to be strong and stoic, but it is essential to recognize and validate your emotions. Growing up without a father may leave you feeling vulnerable and emotionally uncertain at times. It is important to find healthy outlets for expressing and processing your emotions, such as talking to a trusted friend, counselor, or joining support groups.

Music was the outlet for me. I could get lost in the sound of the beat. My first heroes were rap artists like Tupac. His album, "Me Against the World" resonated deeply within my soul. It was as if I wrote the lyrics.

Music still has a way to motivate people. I would just suggest to be careful what a young developing mind is listening to. Artists are not always responsible about what they're rapping, especially in this era. I lot of them talk about their latest drug craze. They're just trying to escape poverty themselves, so they will say most anything to fulfill that desire.

My soul connected with the rhythm of the music that would later inspire my imagination, enabling me to clearly see the vision of what I was supposed to be doing on this planet.

Remember that strength does not lie in oppressing emotions but rather in acknowledging and effectively dealing with them. When a young person just simply tells the truth about what he or she is feeling, it allows a conscientious adult to help properly deal with that emotion. If nothing more, it allows the trapped feelings a way to be released.

Seeking Guidance and Knowledge

As a teenager, it is natural to yearn for guidance on how to become a man and how to scale the world that you are creating for yourself.

Without a father figure, this guidance may seem elusive. However, there are other ways to acquire the knowledge and skills you seek. Engage in self-education by reading books, listening to podcasts, listening to empowering music or watching videos on topics such as personal development, masculinity, and emotional intelligence. Seek out mentors in your chosen field of interest who can offer guidance and advice on career paths and life choices. Remember, the quality of your thoughts are predicated on what you allow to enter into your mind.

Defining Your Own Masculinity

Remember that masculinity is not a one-size-fits-all concept. Society often imposes rigid expectations and stereotypes about what it means to be a man. But it is essential to define your own version of masculinity based on your values, beliefs, and personal experiences. Recognize that being a man is not solely determined by physical prowess or conforming to societal norms, but rather by embodying qualities like integrity, empathy, resilience, and respect for oneself and others.

Embracing Positive Male Relationships

The absence of a father figure can be difficult, but it's important to recognize that there are countless positive male relationships to be formed throughout your life. Cultivate relationships with mentors, friends, and colleagues who can provide guidance, support, and friendship. Surround yourself with individuals who uplift and inspire you, and who embody the values you aspire to. These relationships can help shape your understanding of masculinity and allow you to learn and grow alongside other men.

Developing Self-Reflection and Self-Awareness

Without a father figure to guide you, it becomes even more crucial to develop self-reflection and self-awareness. Take the time to understand your strengths, weaknesses, and values. Reflect on your actions and behaviors, and consider how they align with your vision of masculinity. Engage in activities that promote personal growth, such as journaling, meditation, or therapy. By continuously exploring and understanding yourself, you can develop a strong sense of identity and purpose.

Giving Yourself Permission to Make Mistakes

When there is no father in the home, and you are attempting to fill those masculine shoes or even as breadwinner, as a teenager you may not always have the answers or know the "right" way to handle certain situations. It's essential to give yourself permission to make mistakes and learn from them. Understand that nobody has all the answers, and it's through trial and error that we grow and develop as individuals. Embrace the journey of self-discovery and be compassionate with yourself along the way.

Becoming Your Own Man

Ultimately, the absence of a father figure does not limit your ability to become a strong, compassionate, and successful man. By actively seeking positive male influences, engaging in activities that resonate with your interests, and developing self-awareness, you can forge your own path and define your own version of masculinity. Remember that being a man is not solely about external validation or conforming to societal expectations, but rather about embracing your authentic self and living a life true to your values and principles.

Although unique challenges are presented without a male role model in the home, particularly when it comes to understanding and navigating masculinity but you can overcome these challenges and grow into a confident and well-rounded individual. I don't know who this message is for, but being acutely aware that there are others out there that have grown up without a father and are presently growing up without a father, I had to express it.

Remember that your journey is a special time here on earth and that you have the power to shape your own identity and create a meaningful and fulfilling life, regardless of the circumstances of your upbringing.

Absence Damages the Heart

According to reports on the well-being of children in economically advanced nations, children in the U.S., Canada and the U.K. rank extremely low in regard to social and emotional well-being. Many theories have been explored to explain the poor state of our nation's' children. However, a factor that has been largely ignored, particularly among child and family policymakers, is the devastating effects of a father's absence in children's lives. A father's absence can cause irreparable damage, so give your children the type of healthy home life that will produce productive citizens.

For starters, studies repeatedly show that children suffer greatly without a father's positive influence in the home. Even before a child is born, their father's attitudes regarding the pregnancy, behaviors during the prenatal period, and the relationship between their father and mother may indirectly influence risk for adverse birth outcomes. In early childhood it is well known that school-aged children with good relationships with their fathers were less likely to experience depression, to exhibit disruptive behavior, or to lie. Overall, they were far more likely to exhibit prosocial behavior.

In adolescence, the implications of fatherless homes are incredible, as these children are more likely to experience the effects of poverty.

Former president George W. Bush even addressed the issue while in office, stating, "Over the past four decades, fatherlessness has emerged as one of our greatest social problems. We know that children who grow up with absent-fathers can suffer lasting damage. They are more likely to end up in poverty or drop out of school, become addicted to drugs, have a child out of wedlock, or end up in prison. Fatherlessness is not the only cause of these things, but our nation must recognize it is an important factor."

Many individuals can attest to the fact that the lasting impact of a father in a child's life cannot be denied. Many would admit that they have struggled with feelings of abandonment and low self-esteem, due to the lack of a father's love in their lives. Some have turned to drugs, alcohol, risky sexual activities, unhealthy relationships, or other destructive behaviors to numb the pains of fatherlessness.

Although the absence of their father is not an isolated risk factor, it definitely can take a toll on the development of a child.

According to Psychology Today, researchers have found these narratives to be true. The results of a father's absence on a child are nothing short of disastrous, along a number of dimensions:

• Children's diminished self-concept, and compromised physical and emotional security (children consistently report feeling abandoned when their fathers are not involved in their lives, struggling with their emotions and episodic bouts of self-loathing)

• Behavioral problems (fatherless children have more difficulties with social adjustment, and are more likely to report problems with friendships, and manifest behavior problems; many develop a swaggering, intimidating persona in an attempt to disguise their underlying fears, resentments, anxieties and unhappiness)

• Truancy and poor academic performance (71 percent of high

school dropouts are fatherless; fatherless children have more trouble academically, scoring poorly on tests of reading, mathematics, and thinking skills; children from father absent homes are more likely to play truant from school, more likely to be excluded from school, more likely to leave school at age 16, and less likely to attain academic and professional qualifications in adulthood)

• Delinquency and youth crime, including violent crime (85 percent of youth in prison have an absent father; fatherless children are more likely to offend and go to jail as adults)

• Promiscuity and teen pregnancy (fatherless children are more likely to experience problems with sexual health, including a greater likelihood of having intercourse before the age of 16, foregoing contraception during first intercourse, becoming teenage parents, and contracting sexually transmitted infection; girls manifest an object hunger for males, and in experiencing the emotional loss of their fathers egocentrically as a rejection of them, become susceptible to exploitation by adult men)

• Drug and alcohol abuse (fatherless children are more likely to smoke, drink alcohol, and abuse drugs in childhood and adulthood)

• Homelessness (90 percent of runaway children have an absent father)

• Exploitation and abuse (fatherless children are at greater risk of suffering physical, emotional, and sexual abuse, being five times more likely to have experienced physical abuse and emotional maltreatment, with a one hundred times higher risk of fatal abuse; a recent study reported that preschoolers not living with both of their biological parents are 40 times more likely to be sexually abused)

• Physical health problems (fatherless children report significantly more psychosomatic health symptoms and illness such as acute and chronic pain, asthma, headaches, and stomach aches)

• Mental health disorders (fatherless children are consistently overrepresented on a wide range of mental health problems, particularly anxiety, depression and suicide)

• Life chances (as adults, fatherless children are more likely to experience unemployment, have low incomes, remain on social assistance, and experience homelessness)

• Future relationships (fatherless children tend to enter partnerships earlier, are more likely to divorce or dissolve their cohabiting unions, and are more likely to have children outside marriage or outside any partnership)

• Mortality (fatherless children are more likely to die as children, and live an average of four years less over the life span)

Advantages of a Great Male Role Model

There are enormous advantages that are afforded to children who have active, involved fathers during childhood and adolescence. The Fatherhood Project researched the specific impacts of father engagement during the different childhood development stages.

• Fathers and infants can be equally as attached as mothers and infants. When both parents are involved with the child, infants are attached to both parents from the beginning of life.

• Father involvement is related to positive child health outcomes in infants, such as improved weight gain in preterm infants and improved breastfeeding rates.

• Father involvement using authoritative parenting (loving and with clear boundaries and expectations) leads to better emotional, academic, social, and behavioral outcomes for children.

• Children who feel a closeness to their father are: twice as likely as those who do not to enter college or find stable employment after high school, 75% less likely to have a teen birth, 80% less likely to spend time in jail, and half as likely to experience multiple depression symptoms.

• Fathers occupy a critical role in child development. Father absence hinders development from early infancy through childhood and into adulthood. The psychological harm of father absence experienced during childhood persists throughout the life course.

• The quality of the father-child relationship matters more than the specific number of hours spent together. Non-resident fathers can have positive effects on children's social and emotional well-being, as well as academic achievement and behavioral adjustment.

• High levels of father involvement are correlated with higher levels of sociability, confidence, and self-control in children. Children with involved fathers are less likely to act out in school or engage in risky behaviors in adolescence.

• Children with actively involved fathers are: 43% more likely to earn A's in school and 33% less likely to repeat a grade than those without engaged dads.

• Father engagement reduces the frequency of behavioral problems in boys while also decreasing delinquency and economic disadvantage in low-income families.

• Father engagement reduces psychological problems and rates of depression in young women.

Overall, the impact that fathers and father figures can make is substantial. Just as there are many positive aspects to father involvement, the effects of father absence can be detrimental as well.

Tips for Dads

With a community of fathers that may need some encouragement or effective concepts, I share things that have worked for me. Dads! I emphasize that it is vital that you make every effort to become actively involved in your child's life – whether you live in the same home as them or not.

Great Ways to Create Healthy and Positive Engagement

• If a man is no longer with the child's mother, speak positively to, and about, her. It is so important to be on the same page as their mother about what you desire your role to be, and what that will look like. This is especially important in situations where the relationship is severed through divorce or separation. Be clear and respectful, emphasizing your desire to be an involved father with your child. Also, speak positively about her in front of your child! You may have your disagreements at times, but your child needs to know that you respect their mother. He or she is just as much her child as he or she is yours! Speaking poorly of their mother will only damage your relationship with them.

• Create a vision for fatherhood engagement. Twenty years from now, what do you hope your child will say about you as a father? What do you hope he or she don't say? Answering these questions will help you clarify your sense of purpose as a dad and guide you in important decisions with your own child. How can you get there?

• Be the bridge between your own father and your child. Whether or not you look to your father (or mother) as a model for parenting, the legacy of our parents, for better and for worse, lives inside each of us. This is why it's important to explore and understand your family legacy, particularly your relationship with your father. How will you pass on the positive aspects of your relationship with your father to your own child? How will you avoid repeating the negative aspects of your relationship with your father?

• Establish a ritual dad time. One way to spend positive time with your child regularly is to create a Ritual Dad Time. This is not meant to replace more frequent rituals like taking your kid to school or reading to him or her at bedtime. Get together as father/child at least once a month, if you have more than one child, do this minimally for at least one to two hours and with only one child at a time (this may be difficult for larger families, but it is essential for building a one-on-one relationship). Choose an activity you both agree on. You may allow your child to choose or alternate who decides. We don't recommend executive decisions, except in cases of extreme resistance. Make sure you talk during your time together. Using "action talk" (i.e., shooting baskets or playing video games while talking) is great, but men also need to model face-to-face dialogue for children of all ages. You don't always need a distraction! Be consistent. The ritual does not have to be on the same day each month, but make sure it happens so your child can count on it. Try scheduling your next ritual time at the end of each time together!

• Know your child. Every child craves the interest, attention, and presence of their primary caregivers. They need you to know who they are as unique individuals, not as vessels for our own grand plans or unrealized dreams. By becoming an expert about your child's lives – knowing what a certain look on their face means, the best way to get them to sleep, who their friends are, what they're doing in school, what causes them stress — you send a clear and powerful message that they are worthy of your time, interest and attention.

• Be known by your child. Letting your child know more about you through storytelling is a great way to strengthen your bond. What were you like at your child's age? What mistakes did you make? How did you handle embarrassment? What were your friends' parents like? Not only do stories humanize you and give your child a sense of where he or she comes from, but this can also be an effective way to initiate meaningful dialogue with your child.

Dads everywhere, let's take the "Good Dad" journey!

STAR

Love is a many splendored thing, and measured in a multitude of ways but I truly think that there is absolutely no measurement for unconditional love. Unconditional love is of the kind that endures without ever wavering.

David Harris Jr.

Young people, especially troubled youths, determine in their own minds who they will accept instructions from. As a young boy growing into a young adult, it was hard for me to accept instructions from anyone that I viewed as the authority, even from those within my own family who I felt were acting like an authoritarian.

But when I would see my aunt's lovely smile and feel the warmth of her never-ending love, I knew I was blessed. Aunt Star gently helped me to understand the relevance of family and what it meant to be courageous under any circumstance.

I remember bumping my head on Aunt Star's coffee table, causing it to bleed. She bandaged my wound as best as she could and rushed me to the hospital. When we made it to the hospital, Aunt Star rocked my pain away before the doctor ever saw me.

Although, the doctor put some medication on the wound and covered it neatly with a gauze pad, there was nothing he could do for my real pain, the pain that was in my heart. A pain that would cause me suffering throughout my adolescence but my aunt's comforting and guiding words were always a source of strength.

Her words would resonate deeply within me as I saw the reflection of my dad's love in her eyes. It was a love that knew no bounds, a love that transcended time and space. And in those moments, I realized that Aunt Star embodied that same love, that same unwavering devotion as many said that my dad had.

I would come to know her immense love, that stretched out like the endless ocean as it enveloped me, nurtured me, and made me feel secure. Aunt Star was not just a caretaker; she was a guiding light, a beacon of wisdom. She taught me the importance of compassion, empathy, and understanding.

I understand the love that dad had for my aunt through her expressions of that same type of love towards me. She speaks highly of my dad's unconditional love but one can never know the limits of unconditional love until one realizes there's no bounds to this type of love as I've learned from my aunt's gentle touch.

With most of the men in our family being either dead or in prison as I was growing up, I often found myself sitting on my aunt's couch, receiving instructions on life. Many times, as we sat, the conversation would turn to my dad, and she would tell me what he would do in certain situations. "Your father could prevail over any situation with his calm demeanor," she said softly, her voice filled with nostalgia. "He loved you fiercely, just as he loved everyone around him that he considered family, immediate or extended family. In fact, he loved some of his extended family as deeply as he did his immediate family."

Aunt Star, the epitome of what I felt an aunt should be, often sat beside me with her comforting presence wrapping around me like a warm blanket as she guided me through difficult times. Her love and support saw me through some of the darkest moments of my life.

A sparkle would always occur in her eyes as she spoke of dad. It was during one of those moments that I realized Aunt Star was doing her best to fill his big shoes. She was wearing many hats, the caring and loving nature of a woman while trying on shoes that the man of the house should wear.

During times when I wasn't representing the best version of myself, my aunt gently encouraged me to do better, reminding me of the power of being a wise man. In the quietness of those times, I felt an overwhelming sense of pleasure, knowing I had this wonderful lady to assist me through the difficulties of life. Hers is the love that helped shape me into the person I am today.

She embraced her role as an aunt with unwavering dedication, going above and beyond what was expected of her. Her love was not just a feeling but a verb – a constant act of nurturing, guiding, and protecting.

I can recall the countless times she gave me her listening ear during moments of heartache, providing advice and wisdom in times of confusion, and celebrating my triumphs with genuine joy. She had a unique ability to understand the complexities of life and to instill in me a sense of resilience and self-belief.

As evenings deepened into night, and I was about to be on my way to whatever destination my young mind was wondering off to, Aunt Star would reach out and take my hand in hers, her touch gentle, yet firm, a silent reassurance that she would always be there for me. And in that simple gesture, I felt a surge of gratitude and a sense of responsibility to not do anything to dishonor my family's name.

In her, I found more than just an aunt. I found a confidant, a mentor, and a friend. She is my pillar of strength, a source of comfort, and an image of what love should be. And as I watch her, I know hers is the type of love that will continue to illuminate brightly.

I have always been cautious about who I entrusted with my children.

I worried about the wrong ideologies seeping into their young minds, about the influences that could shape their impressionable hearts. But with Aunt Star, all those worries were never a concern. I knew, without a doubt, that they were in the safest of hands.

What I missed as a rambunctious youth, with my own children I was able to see how Aunt Star truly shined. Her love for them was evident in every interaction, in the way she eagerly greeted them with open arms and a warm smile. They were drawn to her like magnets, sensing the boundless love and acceptance she radiated. Aunt Star had a deep respect for the individuality of each child. She nurtured their unique interests and talents, encouraging them to explore, discover, and grow at their own pace. Whether it is teaching, David my oldest son how to a be good big brother or patiently listening Donovan, my middle child's endless stories, she creates a space where they feel valued and cherished.

It wasn't just Aunt Star's love. Her values also made her a trusted caregiver. She believed appreciating the differences in other people, teaching my children the importance of considering others' feelings and perspectives. She imparted lessons of kindness, urging them to be a source of support and encouragement for their peers.

With my aunt by our side, I'm confident that my children will grow up surrounded by love, kindness, and acceptance. She is a living testament to the power of unconditional love, and I vow to carry her legacy forward, to be the same source of comfort and support for my own children and my nieces and nephews as she has been for me.

The effect of Aunt Star's love on me and my children was immense. She has an innate ability to create a supportive environment for my children – a sanctuary where they can freely express themselves, learn, and grow. She provides a safe space for them to explore their passions and curiosities, never imposing her own ideologies or stifling their individuality. She allows them to be the little humans that they were, discovering their own self-worth as they travel along their course through life.

I often marvel at Aunt Star's ability to balance love and discipline effortlessly. She set clear boundaries and expectations, teaching them the importance of responsibility and accountability. But even in moments of correction, her love remains unwavering. It was a love that nurtures growth and learning, guiding them towards becoming compassionate and resilient individuals.

I've also witnessed Aunt Star's love spread throughout people in the community, and how her friends cherish her. Through her actions, I learned the significance of giving back and the impact of small acts of kindness.

In the presence of Aunt Star, I felt boundless and I know it was her guidance that gave me the proper space to flourish. I experienced a love that was both momentous and unwavering. I felt safe, secure, and free to be my authentic self. It is a gift beyond measure, one that would shape my life and influence my relationships for years to come.

I've grown to know that Aunt Star has a rare gift, her sparkling eyes filled with love, illuminating her face. All these years, she's been a source of inspiration, a role model, a testament to the transformative power of love.

I made a silent promise to myself to strive to embody Aunt Star's love, to be a source of comfort and support for my children, just as she had been for me. I will carry forward her teachings, instilling in my children the values of compassion, empathy, and unconditional love.

Mamo had the foresight to give her children meaningful names. She gave my aunt, the name, Star, a perfect moniker for such a wonderful soul. She has truly been my shining star. The name Michael being synonymous with an angel. My uncle has been like a guiding angel for our family. The name David, meaning dearly loved in Hebrew, seems to be so fitting as the name for my father.

UNCLE DON

As I reflected on my childhood, one person stands out as a pillar of support and guidance in my life – Uncle Don. He is one of the nicest and most genuine uncles a person could ask for. He does little things like commenting on my social media posts with words of encouragement. He has always made me feel wanted and sincerely loved.

I learned from other family members that Uncle Don's shenanigans holds a special place in the memories of my father's formative years. He entered the lives of my father and his older brother, Mike, when they were all still young. Don-Don, as he's often called, just a few years older than my Uncle Mike, found himself thrust into their lives when his father entered into a relationship with their mother, Fannie.

In an instant, Fannie became not just Dave and Mike's mother but Don's as well. The bond between them grew strong, and Don took on the role of a protector for Dave. He embraced this responsibility as an older brother.

The bond between Uncle Don and the two younger boys quickly blossomed. Their time together was filled with playfulness and wild antics, etching memories that would last a lifetime. He shared with me some stories of their adventures, which was often punctuated by laughter and a sense of nostalgia.

As Fannie worked, Don-Don often found himself babysitting. Those were the times when their mischievous adventures began, Uncle Don recounted. Despite the occasional mishap, Don-Don cherished the bond he shared with my dad. He watched over him, always looking out for his little brother.

As one of the first influences in my father's life, he played a significant role in shaping his character and worldview. While their days were often filled with all sorts of experiences, Uncle Don stood as a shining example of male strength and unwavering care for his loved ones.

I've learned through countless stories, that in the eyes of my father, Uncle Don embodied what it meant to be a strong man. He possesses a quiet confidence that commands respect and admiration. Whether it was his physical presence or his unwavering determination, he exuded a sense of strength that left a lasting impression on my father. Through his actions and demeanor, he taught my father the importance of standing tall, both figuratively and literally, in the face of life's challenges.

But beyond his strength, Uncle Don possesses a heart full of love and care. He shares an incredible devotion to his loved ones, and my father was fortunate enough to experience this firsthand. Uncle Don was always there when my father needed guidance or support, offering a listening ear and words of wisdom. His unwavering presence and genuine concern served as a pillar of support during my father's young years.

Despite the mischievous adventures they embarked upon together, Uncle Don still taught my father so many things about responsibility and one being accountable for their actions. He demonstrated the significance of cherishing and protecting those closest to him. His actions taught my father the value of loyalty, compassion, and selflessness. Uncle Don's love was not limited to mere words; it was reflected in his willingness to go the extra mile to ensure the happiness and well-being of those he held dear.

After sharing my own moments with Uncle Don, I definitely understand why my father cherished his time spent with this incredible person. The lessons imparted and the bond forged between us have left an impression on my life. Uncle Don's influence continues to resonate, serving as a reminder of the importance of strength, both physical and emotional, and the immeasurable power of love and care.

My father embodied the qualities he witnessed in his older brother, Don, striving to be a source of strength and support for his loved ones, drawing from the lessons learned during those unforgettable years. And while disobedience may have marred their days, the lasting impact of Uncle Don's influence remains a testament to the profound effect one person can have on another's life.

Uncle Don told me of some of the times, he remembered. "As we grew older, Dave's wild spirit remained, but now he had the means to indulge in his passions. With the abundance of money, he made, he embraced his love for cars, women, and gambling.

Dave's generosity knew no bounds, especially towards his extended family of brothers who had adopted him or whom he had adopted as his own. When they needed help, Dave was always there, willing to lend a helping hand. Whether it was financial support or guidance, he became the anchor for many who sought his wisdom and assistance."

Uncle Don's presence is a constant reminder of the power of family. He taught me what he felt was the true meaning of love, loyalty, and unwavering support. His actions speaks louder than words.

Through the years, the mischievous adventures of their youth transformed into cherished memories as we all now laugh about the times they got themselves in pickles. As Uncle Don reminisced, he said that theirs was an unbreakable bond that could weather any storm.

When tragedy struck on Dave's passing, leaving behind a void that was felt deeply by his loved ones, Uncle Mike had to grieve from the confines of a prison. The weight of the loss was very heavy, and the devastation was shared not only by Fannie but also by Aunt Star. When Mamo had to go identify my dad's body, Uncle Don was alongside her, a source of strength for my grandmother.

In the aftermath of my dad's passing, Uncle Don recognized the impact that Dave had on the lives of those around him. "He was more than just a gambler and a risk-taker; he was a brother, a friend, and a source of support for many. His absence left a void that can never be filled, as grief reverberated through the hearts of those who loved him.

Dave's body was unrecognizable. The fish and elements had deteriorated him," Uncle Don said, his voice trailing off and I knew he was reliving his pain so I gave him a few minutes.

Talking about the loss of my father brought forth a flood of memories for Don-Don. One particular memory that stood out for Uncle Don was the time when they decided to go joy riding. They would seize the opportunity and sneak away with his Pop's car. Ignoring the consequences that awaited on their return, they took off for a time of excitement. However, this escapade took a dangerous turn when Don-Don was speeding down the street and lost control of the car, crashing it against the curbside on 52nd and Avalon. Dad's arm would be injured in the accident.

Don rushed dad to the hospital, his hearts pounding with fear and regret over the ass whipping that was sure to come. The accident left Dave with stitches on his arm, a visible reminder of their youthful recklessness.

Though the situation was undoubtedly serious, it was also a turning point in their bond. My dad discovered that he had a need for speed. And through their misbehavior, the two of them realized the strength of their connection.

As time passed, the boys grew older, and their bond deepened. Uncle Don became an unbreakable thread that wove through their lives, connecting them in a brotherhood built on love, loyalty, and shared experiences. They supported each other through triumphs and failures, celebrated each other's milestones, and offered a shoulder to lean on during the darkest of times.

I look back on my own formative years, and I am grateful for the lessons Uncle Don imparted. He taught me the value of family, the importance of standing by those you love, and the power of a bond that transcends time and circumstances.

To this day, Uncle Don remains a constant presence in our lives. His love and support continue to inspire us, reminding us of the lasting impact one person can have. Their brotherhood born out of their enjoyment for being naughty, stands as a testament to the strength and resilience of family.

As I walk my own mile, I carry the lessons of Uncle Don with me, cherishing the memories and striving to cultivate a bond with my own siblings that reflect the love and loyalty I witnessed firsthand from him.

COUSIN WILLIE

I sat down with Cousin Willie and as he recounted a treasure trove of stories, tears began to fall as he spoke of my dad. As young kids, they were inseparable. They ran down dirt streets, their laughter echoing through the neighborhood. Their youthful exuberance knew no bounds as they navigated the world together, embracing every opportunity for playfulness.

But it wasn't just their shared penchant for mischief that bound them together. They were kindred spirits, understanding and supporting each other dreams, celebrating successes and providing support in times of disappointment. Their bond was forged not only through shared experiences but also through a deep sense of mutual love and respect.

From chasing girls during their teenage years to navigating the uncertainties of young adulthood, my dad and Cousin Willie were partners in fun. They shared a unique brotherhood, one that connected them on a deeper level. Together, they faced life's challenges and celebrated its joys.

It was my dad that introduced Willie to the world of jet-setting, igniting in him a passion for exploration and adventure. Their shared love for travel took them on exquisite vacations all over the U.S., allowing them to immerse themselves in different cultures, taste new cuisines, and create memories that would last a lifetime.

Through my dad's influence, Willie's horizons expanded, and he learned to embrace the fullness of life. The jet-setting lifestyle became a part of their shared legacy, a symbol of the bond they shared and the dreams they dared to chase. Countless times, he talked fondly about my dad's mischievous.

In Cousin Willie's own words, he enlightened me of my dad's country boy life. "I lived in Oak Grove, a small southern town in the northeastern part of Louisiana. There wasn't much to do there, except work hard.

I couldn't wait for summer to arrive so I could see my cousins Michael and David again, especially David. We were around the same age and we were buddies in the pursuit of girls. There weren't many nice, looking girls in Oak Grove, not many people at all. But the prettiest girls would instantly fall for Dave. Some girls that I had been trying to date for years, Dave had absolutely no problem getting them to agree to go on a date with him. I would tease him that it was only because he was from the city and they thought he was going to help them escape small town boredom.

I knew all the nooks and crannies of Oak Grove, even the dark secrets that lurked in the shadows. The town had a history of racial prejudice, where evil intent towards the black community was sadly prevalent. Despite this, my knowledge of the town made me an invaluable guide for the city boys.

Part of the summer would be spent in Terry, Louisiana, an even smaller town in West Carrol Parish, at Big Mama's house. There, our escapades would often lead us into mischief, and more often than not while we were still adolescents, we found ourselves on the receiving end of Big Mama's discipline.

Once, David, in a moment of playfulness, threw a rock at a girl who had a crush on him. Her screams and tears were sure to bring swift retribution from Big Mama. David rushed into the house and padded himself with extra layers of clothes before we received a whipping from Big Mama. She never just whipped one of us. If one was in trouble, all of us were.

As much as David hated to get a whipping, it didn't slow down his mischievous activities. The next thing I knew, David had turned his attention to chasing the white neighbors' cows that were inside a fence in a large pasture across from Big Mama's house. The thrill of the chase seemed to fill your dad with amusement. I didn't understand why. Maybe because I had been around cows all my life and because this was something new for him, he found enjoyment in it.

One day while he was chasing cows, David stumbled upon the neighbor's horses and his eyes sparkled as if he had seen the most magnificent thing in his whole life. The neighbor walked outside from his house, accusing him of trying to steal his horse. A black man could be hung in those parts during that time for just being black. So, being a horse thief would surely get him hung.

Mike and I sat on the fence, not knowing what to do. I thought of running to get Big Mama. But surprisingly, the neighbor gave him a chance to ride. Once David was successfully aboard, the neighbor whacked the horses rear-end, causing it to charge off. He probably thought David would fall off.

But David surprised everyone, including himself I think, by staying aboard the horse. Mike and I cheered him on. The neighbor's evil intent was turned to semi-celebration as David's ability to handle the horse even impressed him. It was in that moment that David discovered a new passion – horseback riding. The rhythmic gallop and the feeling of freedom seemed to resonate deep within him.

Years passed, and after I graduated from high school, David had bought a brand new '81 Cadillac. He drove the car to Oak Grove to pick me up. Of course, he was an instant celebrity. All the girls wanted a chance to be next to him in his fancy car.

For me, the car was a symbol of the dreams we aspired to achieve. We often talked about being rich when we grew up. David's success marked the beginning of a new chapter in our lives.

As David and I drove the 1800 miles to Los Angeles, I knew I was leaving behind the small town that held both fond memories and bitter experiences forever. I was in search of new opportunities and a chance to break free from the limitations that had haunted me far too long.

We drove into the horizon, the wind carrying my thoughts, and I couldn't help but feel a mixture of excitement and apprehension. The road ahead was uncertain, but I was determined to carve out my own path in LA. But little did I know that the adventures and discoveries I had experienced in Oak Grove could have never prepared me for all that awaited me in Los Angeles.

I stepped out of the car at Aunt Fannie's house into a totally different world. Right from the start, I knew everything I had ever learned about the city could be thrown out of the window. Los Angeles operated under a different set of rules. The first thing I had to get used to was gangbangers calling me Cuz or Blood. But the lifestyle we lived was far removed from the one that gangbangers lived. We lived like white millionaires.

Everything was filled with excitement in LA, but I could expect even more excitement when I was with David. I remember once he was flying down a four-lane street, swerving in between cars at extremely high speeds. And right as he zagged from between a car, a bus pulled out in front of us. We were sure to experience a devastating crash. But in a flash, with a slight turn of the wheel, he swooped by the bus, yelling "Yee-haw!" into the wind that was slapping against our faces. I will never forget that day, his yell reminding me of the way Bo Duke sounded on the series "Dukes of Hazard."

And you talk about a man's word being golden. If your dad told you he would do something for you, you could count it done. But it also carried weight with those that would try to violate us in any way. Once I was seeing this girl, not knowing that this gangbanger was claiming her as his woman, and without her consent. He and his homies confronted me about her and I called David. When he arrived, the gangbangers acted like they had been friends forever. But I would learn from David that they hadn't been. When I asked him, what did he tell them. He just said, he told them I was his cousin.

When I heard about the accident, I couldn't believe. Actually, I still can't believe it till this day. The lives of everyone that loved him took a heartbreaking turn on that dreadful day. At the tender age of 26, he departed from this earth, leaving a void in the hearts of all who knew and loved him. The news of his passing sent shockwaves throughout our family.

Though your dad may no longer be physically present, his spirit lives on in the memories he left behind. His laughter still echoes in my heart, and his love continues to guide me.

Listening to my cousin Willie speak fondly as well as sadly about my father, left me melancholy. I knew the loss of my dad was particularly significant for Willie when he said, "I not only lost a cousin but also a confidant, a partner in adventure, and a dear friend.

In the wake of David's departure, the family clung to his memory, cherishing the moments we shared with him. We laughed through tears as we recalled his hilarious antics and shared heartfelt stories that reflected his generous and compassionate nature, keeping his spirit alive. His vibrant personality and enjoyment of life became a source of inspiration for all of us. We carry his legacy within our hearts, striving to embody the qualities that made him so special – his kindness, his adventurous spirit, and his unwavering love for family and friends.

In honoring Dave's memory, we embrace the lessons he taught us. We take full advantage of every moment, we take risks, and we treasure the bonds of family and friendship. We understood the importance of cherishing our loved ones, for life can change in an instant. I vow to keep his memory alive and well in my mind and heart."

Listening to Cousin Willie's story, my heart swelled with a mix of emotions. I mourned the loss of my dad even more, but was grateful for the impact he had on people's lives. Although Cousin Willie's recounting of a vibrant soul extinguished far too soon left me sad, I understood more of who I am and what is expected of me as his son.

Cousin Willie's vow to honor my dad's memory by living a life filled with purpose, love, and a relentless pursuit of happiness struck a chord within me, and I made the same vow.

Through the tales shared by relatives and the remnants of his presence that lingered within our family, extended family and friends, I developed a deep admiration and love for a man I have no memory of, being only two years old when he died.

But in my heart, I carry the torch of my dad's spirit, channeling his adventurous nature and enjoyment for life. I pursue my own dreams with the same type of vigor, embracing each opportunity that come my way. I honor his memory by living a life that would make him proud that his legacy lives on.

Though my dad's time on this earth was cut short, his influence continues to impact and shape our lives. His absence serves as a constant reminder to cherish the moments we have with our loved ones and to make every day worth living.

In the legacy of David Harris Sr., we find the strength to embrace life's challenges, celebrate its joys, and treasure the bonds that hold us together. His story serves as a reminder that even in the face of loss, love and cherished memories can transcend time, ensuring that his spirit will forever be a part of our lives.

DEUCY

David "Black Dave" Harris met Brian "Deucy" Nellum in middle school, and the two of them became immediately inseparable. And I know why my dad loved Deucy so much. He was a character, and he always kept me laughing. I got to personally know him while I was still young. Growing up, I spent considerable time with him and his family. Deucy would transition from heart conditions at age 61. He was the first of my many uncles that I have come to know well.

Deucy would often visit our Ladera Heights home. This is also where me and his son, Bryshon and my cousin La Rue Jr., would form our close-knit bond. During this time, I lived in the city, and was able to see my cousin's and relatives often.

My mother eventually moved us to Chatsworth, which was about a thirty, minute drive from LA in light traffic. But during rush hour, it could take an hour. Traffic or not, Uncle Deucy would take the drive over the hill to make sure that we were okay.

Through Uncle Deucy's stories, my dad became incarnate in my mind and heart. And so many of the stories I've heard over the years from Uncle Deucy rang clear for this re-telling.

After I was told the story about dad bringing Deucy home to live with them, it became one of the most meaningful lessons I've ever learned about family. From that moment, I began declaring that it's not just blood that makes you family, but love and loyalty does also.

As the story goes, Deucy would eventually move in at my Mamo's house. And he would become as much as a brother to Dave as his blood brother Michael was. And he would become as much as a son to Mamo as the two sons she birthed.

Deucy had found a place to call home in Ms. Fannie Jordan's house. The house on 46th and Central became a sanctuary for the trio, a place where they could scheme, plan, and find solace amidst the chaos of the LA streets.

Deucy said from the moment he and Dave met, a deep and unbreakable bond formed between them. Deucy, with his magnetic personality and street smarts, quickly became an integral part of Dave's inner circle. There was an unspoken understanding between him and Deucy, a pact that they would always have each other's backs, no matter what.

The names Dave and Deucy became synonymous. They shared a common vision and an unyielding loyalty to each other. Just like Dave's older brother Michael, Deucy was there through thick and thin, a constant presence in his life. The dynamics of the three boys formed a powerful allegiance as they grew into men, their names identified with power and wealth in the illicit drug trade of 1980s Los Angeles.

Deucy always sounded so proud as he spoke about dad. "Dave created an empire without even trying and it quickly expanded as he amassed great wealth. But his success was not solely driven by personal gain. He craved enjoyment like none other.

In those days, your dad was one of the most trusted men in all of LA. Drug dealers would just drop off their money for cocaine, and Dave wouldn't have any to sell for some times up to three days. The men trusted him so much that they never worried about losing their money. They wouldn't dare leave their money with me or none of the rest of us in our crew.

He became known for his diplomacy, using the gift of gap instead of the power of the gun. His conflict resolution tactics were so uncommon in the violent underworld of criminal politics that they became respected, they even became notorious. He could de-escalate a situation by just showing up with his brilliant smile."

I would learn that it was dad's unwavering loyalty to Deucy that truly defined him. There was nothing he wouldn't do for his brother, and their bond was evident to anyone who crossed their path. When you saw one, you saw the other, two sides of the same coin.

Deucy, with his streetwise demeanor and uncanny ability to handle the treacherous underbelly of their world, became Dave's trusted confidant and partner in crime. They complemented each other perfectly, balancing their strengths and weaknesses. Dave's strategic mind and Deucy's street smarts formed an unstoppable force.

In the volatile landscape of the drug trade, where alliances were fleeting and betrayals were commonplace, Dave and Deucy's brotherhood provided a rock-solid foundation. The empire they built, expanded into other territories as they established their dominance without firing one shot. Their names carried respect with their rivals, and their reputation grew with each passing day.

But amidst the glitz and glamour of their success, they never lost sight of their roots. They remained grounded by the love and support of Fannie and their family. Their mother, wise and resilient, served as a beacon of strength and a reminder of the importance of family, even in the darkest of times.

Through the trials and tribulations, they faced, Dave and Deucy stood side by side, their unwavering loyalty never faltering. They celebrated each other's victories and provided unwavering support during moments of defeat. Their bond was unbreakable, forged in the crucible of the streets and fortified through shared experiences.

In the height of their success, Dave and Deucy basked in the wealth and power of successful men. With success comes a bevy of beautiful women and most any other thing a man desired. But also, with success comes responsibility. And these men were too young to truly understand the consequences of their actions. They were having children out of wedlock, that created broken and dysfunctional homes. And they were doing crimes against the United States that couldn't last.

Deucy told me that he once suggested that they should join a neighborhood gang for the added support. Dave replied, that's not our brand. We're players. How do you think I can go into any neighborhood and not have any problem with anyone. If we chose a side, that will all change.

Most of my life, I was unaware of Uncle Deucy's presence on the boat the day my dad died. It wasn't until I started this book that this information came to light. Deucy was actually the last person to ever see dad alive.

Seeing his brother dying and being unable to do anything about it, had to be very traumatic. So, initially, I didn't specifically ask Deucy about the accident. But when he found out that his brother's story was being created, he stepped up once again for Dave and offered any help he could contribute.

In the retelling of the boating accident, he started by saying, "That day was the worst day of my life." But after he uttered that heartfelt sentence, he just gave me mostly vague information. He only told me the types of things that my mom had already shared with me.

But I wanted details. When I approached Deucy for more information about that day, it wasn't easy for him to relive the event. He choked up every time he tried to explain the actual drowning.

And I knew to continue questioning him would only do more damage than good. But with Deucy's story as my compass, I continued my journey, determined to unearth the truth. The road ahead wasn't anything short of challenging. To have people revisiting a love one's death, some still with raw feelings, was filled with twists and turns. But I knew that I had to keep pushing forward if I were to accomplish my goal.

As I walked this path, I couldn't help but feel a deep connection to the stories about my father's relationship with Deucy. Their stories were intertwined with my own, and I was determined to uncover the truth, not just for the sake of writing this book, but for my own personal closure.

This became a journey that would test my limits, challenge my perceptions, and ultimately shape the person I was becoming as a result of the truth I was discovering.

KERLINE

Mind you, some of the people that I interviewed, I had never met before. And many times, I would meet someone and after their interview, they would refer me to someone else, even sometimes when I asked something that struck a common cord, they would ask me had I reached out to so-and-so? This is how Kerline came to this book project. Until a friend of both my father and her told me of their special bond, I wasn't aware. I knew she had been instrumental in the upbringing of my cousin Mykel, Uncle Mike's daughter but I had no knowledge of the deep relationship she shared with my father.

Just talking with Kerline and hearing the tremendous energy in her voice when she reflected on her times with my father, I could hear the admiration for him coming through the phone line. And to see her, the sparkle in her eyes, leaves no doubt why two people with so much charisma would become friends. The following is how she remembers David Harris Sr.

Kerline's arrival in Los Angeles in 1980 marked a significant turning point in her life. Having recently moved from Brooklyn, New York, where her family settled after leaving Haiti, she brought with her a wealth of cultural experiences and a solid educational background that included fluency in four languages. Eager to pursue her passion for beauty and hairstyling, Kerline found herself working at Liberty Park

Beauty College, where she would cross paths with two individuals who would leave an indelible mark on her life – David and Michael Harris.

It was within the walls of the beauty college that Kerline first encountered the Harris brothers. David, the younger of the two, immediately caught her attention with his striking good looks and captivating smile. His black and lustrous hair, beautifully permed and perfectly styled, became a canvas for Kerline's hairstyling skills. She took great pride in working on his long locks, constantly striving to enhance his already impressive appearance. Kerline spent hours perfecting her roller sets on David's long hair, marveling at the way his locks effortlessly fell into place.

Dave, as Kerline fondly called him, possessed a mischievous and playful nature that endeared him to those around him. He had a unique ability to inject humor into even the most serious of situations, leaving everyone in stitches with his jokes and pranks. His infectious laughter and lighthearted spirit brought joy to those fortunate enough to be in his presence.

Long before society began using terms like "swag," Dave effortlessly exuded an undeniable charm and confidence. He had a keen fashion sense, dressing impeccably in designer clothes every day, leaving a lasting impression wherever he went.

As Kerline and Dave's friendship blossomed, they became like brother and sister. They bonded over shared experiences, dreams, and a mutual understanding of the challenges they had overcome in their respective journeys. They supported each other's ambitions and celebrated their milestones together.

Their friendship blossomed as Kerline spent her days honing her skills at Cindy Lu's, the salon owned by the school, where the two of them would often talk. And there came a time when Dave refused to let anyone else touch his hair except Kerline.

"Dave had a way of lightening the mood, turning serious moments into laughter-filled ones. The girls at the salon adored David, enchanted by his charm and his ability to make anyone feel at ease. He had a natural charisma that drew people in," Kerline recalled.

Kerline's passion for hairstyling led her to open her own beauty salon called Le Chic in Inglewood, a confirmation of her hard work and dedication. Kerline's salon became a haven of creativity, a place where her clients not only received exceptional hairstyling but also felt the warmth in her personality.

When Dave learned of her accomplishment, he made it a point to visit regularly, not only for Kerline's expertise in maintaining his flowing perm but also to show his unwavering support for his friend. He would arrive in exotic cars, evidence of his own burgeoning success, and would always leave Kerline a generous tip, a small gesture that spoke volumes about his character.

Kerline would also have the opportunity to meet Dave's mother, Fannie. It was clear to Kerline that Fannie loved her son deeply, but she also had moments where he seemed to get on her nerves with his playful antics. Kerline recognized the complex dynamics of the love the two of them shared and she marveled in their relationship.

One day while working at Le Chic, she got the news of the boating accident that claimed Dave's life. Shockwaves coursed through Kerline's body, shaking her foundation. The circumstances surrounding the incident were shrouded in uncertainty, as conflicting stories swirled around, but none of that mattered to Kerline. The loss of her dear friend shattered her heart, leaving an enduring void that lingered even to this day.

In the wake of Dave's untimely passing, Kerline found solace in the memories they had created together. She clung to the laughter, the shared experiences, and the genuine connection they had fostered. Dave's absence left an immense void, a constant reminder of the uncertainties of life. Despite the passage of time, Kerline carried Dave's spirit within her, vowing to honor his memory by living each day to the fullest and cherishing her family and friends as he did.

The loss of Dave didn't just affect Kerline personally; it also had a significant effect on the community they were a part of. As news of his passing spread, friends, colleagues, and clients alike mourned the loss of a charismatic and kind-hearted individual who had touched their lives. Kerline's beauty salon became a place of remembrance, as people gathered to share stories, offer condolences, and find comfort in each other's presence.

Michael, devastated by the loss of his beloved brother, would call from prison to lean on Kerline for support, finding solace in their shared experiences and the understanding they had of one another's pain. Together, they maneuvered the difficult journey of healing, cherishing the memories of their time with Dave and finding strength in their enduring friendship.

In the absence of my uncle Mike and amidst the struggles faced by her biological mother, Kerline emerged as a guiding force and nurturer for my cousin Mykel. Her unwavering love and dedication transformed her into a great mother figure, providing the care and support that Mykel needed during this challenging time.

When circumstances prevented Mykel's biological mother from fulfilling her maternal role, Kerline selflessly stepped in to fill the void. With compassion and tenderness, she embraced the responsibility of motherhood, offering Mykel the stability and guidance she deserved. Despite not being her biological mother, Kerline's love for Mykel knew no bounds.

Kerline's presence in Mykel's life was not merely a substitute; she became an anchor, providing a sense of security and a source of comfort.

She created a nurturing environment where Mykel could grow, thrive, and flourish. Kerline's consistent presence and unwavering support allowed Mykel to feel loved and cherished, even in the midst of uncertainty.

Through her actions, Kerline demonstrated the true essence of motherhood. She selflessly gave her time, energy, and affection to ensure Mykel's well-being. Whether it was offering a listening ear, providing guidance through life's challenges, or simply being there to celebrate her achievements, Kerline's devotion and commitment were unwavering.

While my uncle was away, Kerline also played a crucial role in maintaining a sense of family and connection for Mykel. She fostered a loving and inclusive environment, ensuring that Mykel felt a sense of belonging and support. Kerline's efforts were instrumental in bridging the gap and providing a stable foundation for Mykel's emotional and psychological development.

Mykel's journey was undoubtedly shaped by the love and care bestowed upon her by Kerline. Her dedication and selflessness enabled her to overcome obstacles and grow into a resilient and compassionate individual. The bond they developed transcended biology, illustrating the profound impact that a nurturing and supportive figure can have on a child's life.

Kerline's role as Mykel's mother figure is a testament to the power of love, friendship, and the innate ability to create familial bonds beyond blood ties. Her willingness to step into the role of a caregiver exemplifies the strength of her character and the depth of her love for Mykel. Their unique bond serves as a reminder that family is not solely defined by genetics but also by the love and care we extend to one another.

I witnessed firsthand the love the women had for each other at the baby shower that Kerline hosted for Mykel at her house. Mykel said that she is forever grateful for Kerline's presence in her life. Her unwavering support, sacrifices, and unconditional love have helped shape my cousin into the person she is today. As they continue their journey together, their bond serves as a testament to the extraordinary strength and resilience of the human spirit.

The passing of time did not diminish the significant effect that Dave's friendship had on Kerline's life. It changed the way she viewed the world and the people in it. It taught her the importance of seizing every opportunity, of embracing laughter and joy, and of treasuring the bonds we form with others. Dave's spirit continues to inspire Kerline, pushing her to live her life to the fullest and to cultivate meaningful relationships with those around her. His presence, even in absentia, serves as a reminder to find humor in the darkest of moments and to embrace the beauty that life has to offer.

Through her work, she continues to spread joy and kindness, just as David had done during his short time on Earth, forever grateful for the friendship they shared and the impact he made on her life.

ROCK COCAINE A.K.A. CRACK

The Contra war, also known as the Nicaraguan Revolution, took place in the 1980s in Nicaragua. It was a conflict between the Sandinista government, which came to power after overthrowing the Somoza dictatorship in 1979, and the Contras, a counter-revolutionary group backed by the United States.

During the Contra war, the United States government, particularly the administration of President Ronald Reagan, provided financial and military support to the Contras. The U.S. government wanted to undermine the Sandinista government, which it viewed as a Soviet-backed communist regime. But due to legal restrictions and political opposition, the U.S. Congress prohibited direct funding of the Contras.

To bypass these restrictions, the Reagan administration sought alternative means to fund the Contras. One controversial method was the diversion of money from the sale of arms to Iran. If Congress didn't approve funding, how did the Reagan administration secure funds to buy weapons from Iran (with their good looks?)?

Nicaragua, being a major transit point between South America and the United States, the Contras, seeking alternative sources of funding due to restrictions on direct U.S. government support, turned to the multi-billion, dollar cocaine industry. Officials from the United States began either facilitating or directly participating in drug smuggling to generate revenue.

In what became known as the Iran-Contra affair, proceeds from the arms sales were secretly funneled to the Contras in Nicaragua. Reports and investigations would later say that some rogue agents, often operating independently or in small groups, (Fall Guys) engaged in this drug trafficking activities. They facilitated the transport of drugs, particularly cocaine, through Nicaragua and collaborated with drug cartels to create tremendous profits.

These agents distributed drugs in Urban neighborhoods all across America, particularly in South-Central Los Angeles. Before this time, many people say it was literally impossible to find drugs in a black neighborhood, especially a costly drug like cocaine, which was considered a wealthy person's drug of choice. Reports say that there was more than two hundred million dollars extracted from South Central Los Angeles alone to back America's intrusion into other peoples' business.

Two of the most notorious figures linked to the Contras and drug trafficking was Oscar Danilo Blandón, a Contra supporter who became involved in the cocaine trade with U.S. Colonel Oliver North. Blandón claimed that he sold drugs in the United States while North and the U.S. turned a blind eye, and he used the proceeds to purchase weapons and supplies for the Contras. Another individual, American pilot and Contra affiliate Barry Seal, was also involved in drug smuggling operations that reportedly flew in hundreds of thousand tons of cocaine, flooding the U.S. with this illicit product.

The war had unintended consequences that reverberated across the United States. The diversion of funds from the sale of arms to Iran to support the Contras was a violation of U.S. law, specifically the Boland Amendment, which prohibited U.S. government assistance to the Contras, leading to a major political scandal. And distributing cocaine, a Schedule II drug (substances that have a high potential for abuse), violated U.S. drug laws. The Reagan administration argued that it was a necessary and justified action to support anti-communist forces in Nicaragua, while they were ruining the lives of countless Americans.

This war led to the flooding of drugs, particularly tons of cocaine, into the country. The influx of so much of this illicit substance in a very short period of time further exacerbated the drug crisis. With so much powder cocaine available, someone figured out how to create a substance to smoke, which became a popular way to consume the drug. On the West Coast cooked cocaine was called "rocks." It was produced with a simple conversion process. Powder cocaine mixed with sodium bicarbonate (regular cooking baking soda) and dissolved in water and heated until it forms a solid "rock" or "crystal." The rock was removed from the liquid, dried, then broken into chunks.

Ether or ammonia was used to create this substance before the discovery of baking soda. Smokers reported that ether and ammonia left afterburn when smoked while baking soda didn't.

Regardless of which compound was used to produce the rock, it was smoked rather than snorted or injected, which allowed for a faster and more intense high. Using the drug in this manner, spread like a plague throughout urban communities during the 80's. And America was left with a crack cocaine epidemic, and a clean-up effort, which directly contributed to the rise in incarceration rates.

America's propaganda machine kicked into gear. From the West Coast to the East Coast, images began to appear of the worse haggardly looking people in the media that were allegedly addicted to cocaine to illustrate how the drug was wreaking havoc on the country. The term "crack" was popularized from a New York Times article in 1985. In the article entitled, "A new, purified form of cocaine causes alarm as abuse increases," describing crack use in Bronx, New York. Within a year, more than a thousand press stories were published as a result of this article.

By 1985, some West Coast dealers had made their fortune selling rock cocaine. But this article and the resulting wide coverage started an avalanche of myths, giving the government ammunition to sentence black and brown people a hundred times greater than their counterparts that distributed powder cocaine.

This moment had approached my dad and he would seize upon it. One of his friends told me that dad sold crack from the back-window at Mamo's house on 46th and Central. "Dave was ambitious," he said. "And he wouldn't be denied his opportunity to get from underneath poverty, feeling like the drug business was the only game left for him to play. Being minutes from Beverly Hills and Hollywood, and seeing so many with so much when he had very little, caused the determination that would change those odds at whatever the cost."

Amongst dealers, this era is called the Golden Era. It marked a glorious time in the lives of young black men and women that indulged in this risqué lifestyle. For the first time in their lives, they had enormous amounts of money, and they didn't have to scrub anyone's floor or slave in a factory to get it.

They were living in upscale neighborhoods and riding around in exotic cars they bought with cash money, and only after a few months of selling their product. Crack cocaine rapidly infiltrated the urban neighborhoods, leading to a wave of violence, addiction, and social upheaval that would leave an ugly stain on these regions.

With so much of the product available, the cost decreased significantly, making it easily accessible to individuals from various socioeconomic backgrounds that couldn't even imagine buying this drug before the Iran-Contra affairs. These affairs, and Reagan's insistence to be involved in the politics of a foreign country, an insignificant third world foreign country, created an enormous amount of tragedy in the

U.S. Remnants of that era still affect many people's lives in adverse ways, such as having to recover for senseless times spent in prison.

The accessibility led to the surge in drug trafficking and the formation of powerful street gangs that vied for control over the lucrative crack trade. Gang violence escalated, resulting in an alarming increase in homicides. Neighborhoods once known for their vibrant communities became battlegrounds plagued by fear and instability.

Dad's friend said, "Every day of the week, smokers would fill the street as his employees sold them cocaine. Dealers were escaping their current reality by becoming rich while others were escaping theirs by staying intoxicated on the drug that the crack dealers sold."

The rise of crack cocaine in Los Angeles brought about the emergence of locations called "spots," which were alternatively named crack houses on the East Coast. Spots became hubs of drug activity where dealers operated and made substantial profits. Crack houses, typically located in impoverished neighborhoods, served as central locations for the sale and/or consumption of crack cocaine. They were characterized by their secretive nature, often hidden in plain sight within residential areas. These houses became notorious for their constant flow of customers, as crack addictions rapidly spread throughout the city.

The impact on the healthcare system was significant as well. Hospitals and emergency rooms were overwhelmed by the influx of crack-related medical emergencies, including overdoses, violence-related injuries, and the spread of infectious diseases associated with drug use.

It is crucial to recognize that these events were not isolated incidents but rather reflections of larger societal issues. America, struggling with the consequences of the tons of cocaine left on her streets, the aftereffects of funding an unapproved war left her with a crack cocaine epidemic, causing far-reaching implications for law enforcement and the criminal justice system.

The government responded with aggressive anti-drug policies. The convergence of this personal tragedy, changing drug laws, and the consequences of geopolitical conflicts created a perfect storm of turmoil and upheaval. The government had to figure out some way to clean up their mess. So, they created a "black sheep," a young black or brown person from urban communities. Her best idea to solve this self-inflicted problem was to go to war with her minority population and call it the "War on Drugs."

Someone in Congress got the bright idea to punish crack cocaine dealers with sentences a hundred times greater than the sentences powder cocaine dealers were receiving and to make sure they were in prison a very long time, they enacted mandatory minimum sentences, resulting in a person convicted of a drug crime to have to serve 85% of their sentence before they had any possibility of being released. The 100 to 1 disparity in Federal sentencing had a disproportionate impact on minority communities, particularly African Americans.

The harsher penalties for crack cocaine offenses led to a significant increase in the incarceration rates of African Americans, who were more likely to be involved in crack cocaine-related offenses. This contributed to the overrepresentation of minorities in the criminal justice system, disproportionately affected marginalized communities and perpetuated racial disparities in incarceration, resulting in what we now know as "mass incarceration."

The sentencing disparity reflected and reinforced racial biases within the criminal justice system. The perception that crack cocaine was associated with inner-city minority communities and powder cocaine with more affluent users led to discriminatory enforcement and prosecution practices. This resulted in African Americans facing harsher penalties compared to their white counterparts for similar drug offenses.

The 100 to 1 ratio had a profound impact on minority communities. Lengthy prison sentences disrupted families and communities, leading to social and economic instability. Individuals with felony drug convictions faced significant barriers to employment, housing, and education, making it more challenging for them to reintegrate into society after serving their sentences.

The sentencing disparity, highlighting the unequal treatment of different forms of the same drug reinforced the perception of a racially biased criminal justice system and contributed to public distrust and dissatisfaction.

After men and women from the minority community had been incarcerated for a significant portion of their lives, the impact of the 100 to 1 disparity on minorities was widely criticized as discriminatory and unjust. Advocacy groups, civil rights organizations, and policymakers advocated for sentencing reform to address these disparities and promote fairness and equality in the criminal justice system. The subsequent reforms, such as the Fair Sentencing Act of 2010 and the First Step Act of 2018, aimed to reduce these disparities and mitigate the negative effects on minorities.

For more than two decades after mandatory minimum (serving 85% of a sentence replacing parole) and the 100 to 1 ratio was voted into law, black men and women that were severely affected by these ruthless laws that only targeted urban communities, would be trying to defeat these backward sentencing policies. This was an especially troubling time for young black and brown children, causing them to grow up without male guidance.

Many of my uncles were taken away for over two decades, some three decades. America finds herself on the wrong side of history in her dealing with the problem she created. Even her convincing propaganda machine can't put a positive spin, not even an acceptable spin, on the complete annihilation of the family structure in minority homes. What she has perpetrated on the dark races is nothing short of genocide.

After so many lives were destroyed, community organizations and grassroots movements finally regained their voice and emerged to address the root causes of addiction and violence, advocating for drug rehabilitation programs, education, and social support networks. Ultimately, the crack epidemic in urban communities during the early 1980s serves as a tragic example of how the proliferation of a powerful and highly addictive drug can ravage a community, perpetuate cycles of poverty and violence, and leave lasting scars on individuals and society as a whole. It stands as a stark reminder of the complex and multifaceted challenges posed by drug abuse and the importance of comprehensive approaches to prevention, treatment, and community support.

It also serves as an example of what happens when a cross-section of the greater community of Americans feel left out of wealth distribution. This is what happens in any society when a cross-section of the community feel like they are not getting their slice of the pie.

Not being included in the wealth distribution in this country, was the reason for my father and young black men to ever start selling drugs. They wanted more, they wanted to taste the wealth that their white counterparts enjoyed. In the consensual transaction of helping someone that was seeking to get high to find their drug of choice, they became very wealthy and at the same time, our country made them the "Black Sheep," enemy number one.

Many of these men were sentenced to life in prison. Before this time, this type of sentence was only given to someone that had the audacity to take another person's life. For the first time in the history of the recorded world, thousands of black and brown men would find themselves locked away forever for only non-violent crimes.

Some of these men were inherently good people, albeit from

dysfunctional homes, homes that provided the best upbringing that they could with the resources available to them. Friends of my father said if a neighbor was unable to pay their bills, he would give them the needed cash. If an old lady in the neighborhood was struggling to get her grocery bags home, he would assist her with the bags or either have one of his boys help her.

For many of the men that participated in the drug trade of the 80's, the emergence of crack cocaine and the ability to have so much when they were accustomed to so little, was too good to be true, making it ultimately impossible for some of them not to get involved.

ROGUES

During this turbulent period in American history, some cops became rogue, taking drugs and money from dealers, locking them up, then redistributing the drugs to dealers that worked for them. And in other instances, a cop would be labeled a rogue, having to take the fall for the greater good of protecting those higher in rank, also known as "Fall Guys."

One such notorious rogue cop, the kind that wasn't a Fall Guy, was J.C. Miller, an officer from Lennox's Southwest Task Force. Miller was known to brutally beat dealers and even their wives and girlfriends. He would arrest a dealer, confiscate his drugs and money, and keep a portion for him and his team.

After six months of this unethical activity, Miller's nefarious deeds would eventually catch up with him and he was arrested. It was reported that he had a Ferrari Testarossa, a speed boat and a mansion in the hills.

Other officers during this time played right on the fringes of ethical. Officer Goldberg and his partner worked out of Parker Center and they patrolled the Low Bottoms, the area where my dad grew up. As the name Black Dave began to ring, every chance Goldberg got he was searching his pockets without a search warrant, which is an illegal practice in violation of a person's Fourth Amendment rights.

Dave was so loved by the community that if police was surveillancing his spot, more than a few people would alert him. On one such occasion, a neighbor called to report that the police were congregating in a parking lot down the street, looking like they were about to carry out a raid, and Uncle Deucy took the product and buried it in the Pit Bull cage.

Law enforcement all over America was using all sorts of illegal practices and were able to get away with it under the guise of protecting the community. Constitutional laws were being violated, cops initiating searches without a probable cause, which is very much illegal. Police would use silly reasons like he just looked like a drug dealer and I pulled him over. How can you just look like a drug dealer? Is it by just being black?

Courts of law were agreeing with these illegal searches, especially when drugs were found. The proper way to handle an illegal stop is not to make the stop without probable cause, meaning the cops should have undeniable evidence that a crime in in progress.

But even after this illegal stop is executed, anything confiscated, even an illegal substance, should have been given back to the owner. Now, as a result of this knowledge, the owner of the substance would become a suspect. A search warrant should have been obtained sometime in the future to search where the suspect resided.

Drug dealers that didn't know or understand their rights were being hauled off to jail, and their public defender (a lawyer paid by the government) was getting them to plead guilty to lengthy prison sentences. And if there was anyone else to tell on, the lawyer was convincing them that the best route to a shorter sentence, was to snitch.

On the local LA scene, some mastermind concocted a machine to knock down walls, destroying houses and anyone behind that said wall. This invention was called the Battering Ram. The Battering Ram was a formidable machine, designed to drive through crack houses, a tool employed by LAPD to forcefully enter properties suspected of being involved in drug trafficking and other criminal activities. This extreme measure was what law enforcement insisted that they needed to combat the spread of cocaine.

The concept behind the mobile ram was straightforward but very controversial. It was essentially a modified military vehicle, reinforced with heavy steel plating, capable of crashing through walls, doors, and barricades. The LAPD stood behind its purpose, declaring that this vehicle was the required weapon to surprise and overwhelm suspects, minimizing the potential for armed resistance and ensuring swift apprehension.

Just the sight of the mobile Battering Ram in action was terrifying and utterly ridiculous. With its reinforced front end and powerful engine, it would accelerate towards its target, crashing through anything in its path. The noise and destruction it caused were intended to create shock and disarray among those inside the crack houses, allowing law enforcement officers to enter quickly and apprehend.

While the intentions behind the ram were rooted in the urgency to combat the crack cocaine epidemic, its use raised significant ethical concerns. Eventually, critics argued that the machine's destructive power went beyond what was necessary for law enforcement purposes. It posed a risk to innocent individuals who might be present in targeted locations, and the collateral damage caused by its forceful entry was substantial.

On a number of occurrences, police drove the Battering Ram through residential locations that were not crack houses. On one such occasion, a mother and her three children were eating ice cream and watching cartoons. Just imagine the fear they faced, seeing a machine breaking down their wall.

Over time, public outcry and legal challenges prompted a reevaluation of the mobile Battering Ram's use. Recognizing the potential for abuse and the violation of civil liberties, lawmakers and law enforcement agencies revisited their strategies for combating drug-related crimes with this vehicle. Even in the face of a devastating drug crisis, commonsense legislators realized that the methods employed to combat the problem must be balanced with respect for individual rights and the preservation of community trust. Eventually, the use of the mobile Battering Ram was outlawed, and alternative methods were sought to address the crack cocaine epidemic.

We should hold our elected officials accountable for such absurd measures. The mistakes of the past should teach our officials how to utilize more compassionate and effective approaches to address drug-related issues. The lessons learned from the crack cocaine era should guide us in building a safer, more equitable future, where the well-being and dignity of individuals and communities are at the forefront of our efforts.

The outlawing of the mobile Battering Ram in response to the crack cocaine epidemic marked a critical moment of reflection and reform for law enforcement agencies in Los Angeles. It forced a reassessment of tactics and a deeper examination of the root causes behind the drug crisis that had gripped the city.

The devastating impact of crack cocaine on communities, particularly marginalized neighborhoods, could not be ignored. It became evident that a more comprehensive approach was needed, one that went beyond merely targeting drug houses and making arrests. After many years, law enforcement agencies began to shift their focus towards prevention, rehabilitation, and community engagement.

But it won't be until our officials understand that we will always have drug epidemics as long as complex factors such as poverty, systemic inequality, and lack of access to education and healthcare, exist. To address the underlying issues that contribute to drug abuse and addiction, law enforcement agencies should collaborate more with community organizations that live with the problem every day.

Officers should be required to live in the neighborhood that they police and encouraged to engage with residents, listen to their concerns, and work collaboratively to develop strategies for crime prevention and intervention. This will build trust and establish meaningful relationships between law enforcement and the communities they served.

More investments need to be made in drug treatment programs, education, and job training opportunities, providing individuals with alternatives to a life of crime and addiction. The focus has to shift from punitive measures to rehabilitation and support, recognizing that breaking the cycle of drug abuse requires a multi-faceted approach.

The lessons learned from the devastating era, should guide us to a more compassionate and holistic approach to law enforcement. And while we're at it, can we strip "Police" from their title and began to call them "Peace Officers." Just the connotation of Peace Officer sounds and feels better.

A peace officer's duty will be to only keep the peace, not brutalize or kill anyone. A peace officer should get sensitivity training on how to deal with citizens, especially a soldier who works for law enforcement after returning from any type of conflict where he's been trained to kill the enemy. He or she should be taken through a series of psychological tests to determine if they can recognize a citizen from the enemy.

We need swift and effective police reforms to inform them how to do their intended purpose, the protection of civil liberties, and the importance of maintaining a sensitive balance between public safety and individual rights. Our drug problem or any societal problem will never be solved through brute force. The dangers of unchecked power and the need for accountability within law enforcement will remain as long as they wear the Police badge. The pursuit of justice should always be tempered with empathy, understanding, and a commitment to uplifting communities.

It took thirty years for state and federal legislators to change these backward policies. I was grateful that the change finally helped my Uncle Mike to get released. But we need to realize the facts that America's policies are draconian. A person sitting in prison for the distribution of marijuana is beyond ridiculous. Any person that has committed a non-violent crime, for whatever drug offense, should never have to face the rest of his/her life in prison.

In the aftermath of the crack cocaine era, Los Angeles became a testing ground for innovative strategies aimed at addressing societal issues from a broader perspective. The city's experience prompted other law enforcement agencies across the country to reevaluate their own tactics and seek more progressive and community-oriented approaches to public safety.

While the scars left by the crack cocaine epidemic may never fully fade, the reforms that emerged from this dark period paved the way for a broader discussion, which we are still having at the time of this publication.

Every productive citizen's desire is to live in a thriving community, to raise their children in a safe environment. As we move forward, it is imperative to remain vigilant in our efforts to oversee the actions of our elected officials. It's our responsibility to ensure that they continue to prioritize compassion, equity, and community collaboration. This is how we build a more inclusive society where all citizens can know that they are welcomed in the greater America, that their future is filled with as much promise and opportunity as the next citizen.

The effects of the crack epidemic were not limited to the 1980s, its legacy continues to shape the social, economic, and cultural fabric of urban communities until this date.

Let's begin to work towards a more compassionate and equitable future. Let's demand that reforms are made in drug policies, criminal justice, and social programs. These are necessities to address the injustices perpetuated on the dark races.

Let this ugly period and others like it serve as not only a reminder of the profound impact of a "non-sense" law or violation of the law by those elected to enact laws and those paid to uphold the laws can cause, but also let it serve as a reminder to never let this happen again.

Let's never again be so narrow-sighted not to see the effects that historical events like the Nicaraguan War, the catalyst for cocaine flooding into America, can have on an entire nation. All of these very serious offenses happening right under our noses, should serve as a call to action, urging you to examine our systems, challenge oppressive structures, and work towards a more just and empathetic society.

Let this writing be your wake-up call. Let's always question societal structures and institutions. Let's hold our politicians responsible for their decisions to enact non-sense laws by swiftly and decisively voting them out of office.

HIP-HOP

Being a "Crack Era" baby, born in 1986, my peers and I were fascinated with the era in history in which we were born, from the popular movie "New Jack City" to the rap we heard and often imitated. The raw lyrics were telling the stories of what happened on the streets of those times, greatly influencing my generation. This is the music that was in my headphones while I was growing up. This music was in my headphones when I decided I would be a record executive.

The crack cocaine epidemic swept through inner-city neighborhoods, leaving devastation and despair in its wake. Yet, amidst the chaos and struggle, a powerful movement was emerging – one that would redefine music, fashion, and art for generations to come. This movement was none other than Hip-Hop.

Hip-Hop, with its roots in the South Bronx of New York City, became the voice of a generation. It provided an outlet for the marginalized and the oppressed, offering a platform for self-expression and cultural resistance. The crack era, with its harsh realities and social upheaval, provided the fertile ground from which Hip-Hop would flourish.

Songs that were created to celebrate the audacious attitude of young black drug dealers, the new rulers of their communities. They introduced a new swag to the world, showcasing proudness as they stood tall in the advent of their financial success.

But with what we know today, America created her own gangster movie. If it had not been for American planes or American sponsored planes, the amounts of cocaine that reached these shores, never would have been. And the facts for this movie wouldn't be available.

The collective energy of young drug dealers created a world that people had never seen before. Many drug dealers would invest in this new art form. From the Crack Era sprung Hip Hop culture – it's roots firmly embedded in the Crack Era, from companies being started with drug money to rappers' lyrics glorifying the lifestyle.

As crack cocaine ravaged communities, it created a sense of urgency and desperation. The youth, disillusioned by the lack of opportunities and the systemic injustices they faced, turned to music as a means of escape and empowerment. Hip-Hop, street music, became their voice. The music of their reality became their weapon against a world that seemed determined to keep them down.

This era witnessed the rise of a very lucrative drug culture that deeply influenced various aspects of society, particularly in urban communities. This counterculture was a society of young men and women, mostly black, that lived on the fringes of society and made their own rules and abided by their own laws. Their rebel attitude heavily influenced the lyrical content of Hip-Hop music. Artists often rapped about the dangers, and consequences of the drug use, reflecting the realities they witnessed firsthand. Songs like "White Lines" by Grandmaster Flash and Melle Mel and "Straight Outta Compton" by N.W.A. tackled the drug trade, addiction, and the impact of drugs on communities. These narratives served as social commentary, bringing attention to the issues surrounding drugs and amplifying the voices of marginalized communities.

As a young man, learning life through my own awful mistakes, I gravitated to songs like "Keep Your Head Up" by Tupac. All songs like this resonated with my turbulent emotions, mirroring my young mentality in so many ways that I sometimes felt like they were rapping about my life.

Jay-Z's "Blueprint 1, 2 and 3" often made me think of my father because Jay seemed to exemplify dad's type of swag. Other Jay-Z records was a window into who I wanted to be, strengthening my resolve, or a song like "Run this Town" would serve as an adequate example of what it would take to reach the top.

What was more alluring for most my age, was when artists rapped about mansions and Benzes, and exotic women – all logos of the Hip-Hop brand. The influence of drug kingpins had popularized a distinct street aesthetic that celebrated luxury and excess. This aesthetic was characterized by flashy outfits, oversized jewelry, and designer brands, which also included elements like baggy clothing, tracksuits, and gold chains. This fashion reflected the street culture and the desire for status and recognition within the drug trade.

This culture played a pivotal role in the development of streetwear and branding. Icons of the drug trade became influential figures in urban communities, and their style and fashion choices were emulated by many. Brands like Adidas, Nike, and Kangol gained popularity as symbols of urban fashion, with artists often referencing and showcasing these brands in their music videos and performances. The fusion of street culture, drug culture, and fashion created a unique aesthetic that resonated, shaping the attitudes and aspirations of individuals within urban communities.

It had a far-reaching effect on the lifestyle and attitudes of young followers. The pursuit of wealth, the allure of the fast life, and the desire for material possessions became prominent themes. The drug trade presented an alternative means of achieving success and status, leading to a fascination with the lifestyle of drug dealers. This influence manifested in lyrics, music videos, and the overall mindset of many artists and aspiring individuals, often blurring the lines between reality and fantasy.

While the drug culture of the 80s influenced Hip-Hop, fashion, and lifestyle in various ways, it also served as a backdrop for social and political commentary. Hip-Hop artists used their platform to shed light on the systemic issues that perpetuated drug abuse and the socio-economic inequalities that fueled the drug trade. Classics songs like "The Message" by Grandmaster Flash and the Furious Five and "Fight the Power" by Public Enemy addressed the root causes of the drug culture, calling for social change and justice.

The impact this era had on urban communities are still evident today, particularly those heavily affected by drug abuse and violence. While Hip-Hop artists brought attention to these issues through their music, they also became influential figures who provided an outlet for expression and empowerment. Artists like N.W.A., for example, used their music to shed light on police brutality, racial profiling, and the social conditions that contributed to the drug epidemic. This gave a voice to marginalized communities and sparked conversations about social injustices.

While the explicit glorification of drug dealing has toned down over time, the themes and aesthetics born out of that era continue to shape contemporary Hip-Hop music, fashion trends, and cultural expressions. Artists still incorporate elements of streetwear, urban aesthetics, and social commentary in their work, paying homage to the roots and history of the culture.

Despite its origins in a challenging and often turbulent era, Hip-Hop provided hope and a sense of unity. It became a vehicle for storytelling, a means of preserving history and sharing experiences. Through Hip-Hop, marginalized communities found solace, empowerment, and a sense of belonging.

As the crack era began to fade, Hip-Hop continued to evolve. It transcended boundaries, crossing racial, cultural, and geographic divides. It became a global phenomenon, spreading its influence to every corner of the world. Hip-Hop artists like Tupac Shakur, The Notorious B.I.G., and Jay-Z became cultural icons, our Super Heroes. Other artists such as Professor Griff, a member of Hip-Hop group Public Enemy, used their platforms to address social issues and inspire change.

Today, Hip-Hop stands as one of the most influential and commercially successful genres of music. It has become a cultural force, shaping popular culture and serving as a powerful tool for social commentary. It has given rise to countless subgenres, from conscious rap to trap music, each representing a unique facet of the Hip-Hop movement.

The crack era may have been a time of darkness and despair, but from its ashes emerged a cultural phenomenon that continues to impact the world. Drug dealers' swag is stamped all over this culture, and the music born from it.

Although the movement blossomed from the South Bronx, LA and the West Coast had their own brand of Hip-Hop as did the dirty south when they came to the party. This musical genre founded in 1973 will celebrate 50 years of being in existence this year. Critics said it wouldn't last, now it's an integral part of everything American as well as globally. Hip-Hop, born out of struggle, withstood. Hip-Hop forever!

While the drug culture had both positive and negative impacts, it also provided a platform for social and political commentary, sparking conversations about systemic issues and social injustices. Today, the legacy of the 80s drug culture lives on through the continued evolution of Hip-Hop, fashion, and cultural expressions that draw inspiration from that era.

Will we continue with the same ole status quo or, will out of this era, an outpouring of genius be realized. Will our collective energy produce a stream of consciousness that flows richly with the inclusion of all brilliant thoughts.

The future is calling, how will we answer?

LIL ROB

As soon as Cousin Rob began discussing his relationship with my dad, it was evident that he was a storyteller with his own unique way with words. I was captivated as I listened to his deep voice resonating a sense of understanding his place in the world.

He recounted tales about my father, and my heart swelled with both pride and a tinge of sadness. My dad's untimely passing, more than thirty years ago, still weighed heavily on his soul as it did everyone that loved him.

"Dave had called and asked Willie and I did we want to come to Los Angeles. Hell yeah, we did. When he pulled up in that big bad purple Cadillac, it was as if Heaven had arrived. My cousin driving around in a luxury car like that, gave me an indescribable pride.

Dave visited with his lady friends in Oak Grove for a couple of days, then we pulled out. As soon as we hit the open highway, I felt like I was on the road trip of my young life. I didn't know what to expect in LA nor anything about the new life Dave was living, but I was anxious to find out. From our small town in Louisiana to the big city of Los Angeles was a three-day ride but every minute of our journey felt magical.

And as I stepped out of the Cadillac onto LA soil, I was ready for whatever was next. My nineteen-year old mind knew no boundaries, and whatever my cousin was doing to become wealthy, was what I would be doing."

Rob's stories as did many of the other people's stories became a lifeline for me. With each story, I was becoming better informed about the man responsible for my being on earth. The stories were keeping my father's memory alive in my heart and by documenting them, I had a way to share him with my younger family members, share him with the world. As Rob was describing some of their daring exploits, I could hear my dad's laughter echoing through the years.

"Dave's charm and the way he lived life on the edge was the two things that I loved most about him. It was always so exciting to be around him. I remember your father pulling up one day in a brand-new red Ferrari, affirming his love for speed and style. He asked me to come take a ride with him and without any hesitation, I hopped in. The mighty engine roaring beneath us, becoming the center of attention as we cruised through the streets of Los Angeles. The wind whipped through Dave's permed hair as we sped through the neighborhood. I was already on the thrill ride of my life, so this was just more amenities.

As Cousin Rob was bringing my father's spirit to life in his tales, expressing their adventures with such vividness, I could almost feel the wind in my hair.

"Dave's larger-than-life persona, handsome smile, and undeniable charm, turned heads wherever we went. But now riding around in a Ferrari, they were breaking their necks to see who we were, creating a sense of exhilaration that was uniquely ours. He was one of few black men in the entire city with an exotic car like that. And I felt so privileged to be riding alongside him.

Dave shifted the car into high gear in his usual speed demon manner, and it seemed like we flew out of the Low Bottoms, as our hood was affectionately called. We were quickly down a block and out of the area as he swerved between cars. In no time, we were all the way across town.

The car darted down a block and as we turned the corner, a huddle of girls began yelling his name. I often kidded with him about all the cheerleaders he had.

Dave hopped out with his usual bouncing walk, a walk that announced he had arrived in all the ways a black man in those times prayed to arrive. I followed him over to where the young ladies were standing in a yard. He kissed the prettiest of them on her cheek, whispered something in her ear that caused a giggle, and we were off, his gait bouncing back to the car. As soon as I shut the car door, Dave fishtailed out of the area and zoomed toward the freeway.

Dave rushed passed cars, asking me, which one of them did you like?

The one you kissed on the cheek.

She's mine.

I asked him, why did you ask me then?

Dave laughed in his chuckling way and said, so, you could tell me which of the other ones you liked, fool.

We passed a line of cars like they were standing still as we both were still laughing. All of sudden, smoke began to come from the hood of the car, then it caught on fire. He quickly pulled over and we rushed out of the car. As we watched his beautiful car burn, Dave realized that he had left the emergency brake on.

After a long while, a fire truck arrived and extinguished the burning car. His beautiful car was ruined. A few minutes later, one of Dave's lady friends picked us up. The two of them said goodbye to me back at the spot on 46th and Central.

The next morning Dave pulled up in a red Ferrari, honking the horn. I walked out of the house, asking, how did you get it fixed so fast?

Dave offered his customary chuckle, I bought a new one this morning."

When I thought about this, I couldn't even imagine the type of money it would take to feel comfortable after burning up one Ferrari to purchase another one the next day. Rob's stories added a layer of knowledge as well as another level of interest to my already intrigued mind as he continued.

"The city became our playground, every square mile of it, from the glitz and glamour of Hollywood to the beach scenes to Beverly Hills to all the hot spots in the hood. Hanging out with your father, was like getting the surprise in a Cracker Jack box.

We would take Mulholland Drive to his house in the valley, zooming through the twisting and winding roads as we viewed the stunning city lights below. We indulged in late-night eating, savoring every different kind of food that Los Angeles produced. We would shop in Beverly Hills in the afternoon and be in attendance at a hood street race that night.

We would spend a day on the water, Jet skiing and enjoying each other's company and the company of whichever girls were with us. We held the entire world in the palm of our hands. And we enjoyed the very best of what it had to offer, every single day.

One day, I saw your dad counting 100 thousand really fast like a money counter. From that day, I began calling him Bill.

Amid all the excitement, Dave never forgot the importance of family. He knew Willie and I were just getting established in Los Angeles and he made sure to take care of the both of us with whatever we needed.

Then he and Willie's friend, Tommy, followed us from Oak Grove about a year later. Willie and Tommy drove the eighteen-hundred-mile trek in Dave's purple Cadillac back to Los Angeles just like the three of us had.

Your father and Big Tommy, Rob said, his voice carrying a mix of pride and respect, "They were cut from the same cloth. Loyal to the tee. If you ever needed anything, you could ask either of them, and they'd move heaven and earth to make it happen. That's just the kind of men they were."

Cousin Rob emphasized the unique connection he had with my father and Tommy. "If I ever needed a little financial help, they were the two people I would turn to, their willingness to go the extra mile for those they cared about was without condition."

According to Cousin Rob, my dad and Big Tommy were kindred spirits. Their personalities meshed effortlessly, creating a bond that went beyond friendship. They were brothers in all but blood, united by a deep understanding of escaping poverty by any means necessary. Theirs was the joy of youthful freedom, echoing through the halls of time.

Through Rob's words, I learned about the unbreakable bond they all shared, the camaraderie that ran deep in their crew, and the unwavering support they offered one another. His words painted vivid pictures as he took me back to a time their crew was inseparable. "Our crew was topnotch and untouchable! Nobody in the city ran up on us.

But of all the members in our crew, I was closest with Black Dave and Big Tommy. They always made me feel like family.

Tommy and I were cruising one day when we met Yolanda and Valerie. They were in our hood, waiting for the bus, and we pulled up to the curb and asked them if they needed a ride. To our surprise, they hopped in.

Valerie got in the front seat next to Tommy and Yolanda got in the back with me. We got to know each other on the way to where Yolanda lived with her parents in Windsor Hills. Both girls were a couple of years younger than us, having just finished high school.

After we dropped them off, Tommy said he had his eye on Yolanda and asked had I gotten her number. Of course, I had. When he asked me for it, I didn't hesitate to give it to him. I liked the way Valerie looked anyway. So, we exchanged numbers and Yolanda would become the mother of Tommy's first son, Tierre."

Listening to Cousin Rob's stories, left me with a sense of admiration. It was evident that their crew's relationships were built on trust, respect, and an unspoken commitment to always be there for each other.

I have come to realize that the passing of time does not diminish the love we hold for those who have left us. Instead, it deepens our appreciation for the impact they had on our lives. The pain of their absence may linger, but so does the gratitude for having known them. I love that I have taken the opportunity to share in those moments through my dad's family and extended family.

Today, I carry Black Dave's legacy within me, a torch passed down through the ages. As I navigate the waters of life, I am comforted by the knowledge that my father is looking down upon me, his chuckle echoing through the wind, reminding me to seize every moment, to cherish every relationship, and to live a life worthy of his memory.

BIG TOMMY

Several people that I had interviewed kept mentioning Big Tommy's name, and expressing how close he and my father were. His name had surfaced so frequently that I began to ask if anyone had his contact information. No one did.

One day as I was interviewing, Uncle Whitey, he asked, "Have you met your Uncle Tommy yet?" When I said, "No," he immediately got him on the phone.

Tommy and I met for coffee the next day at a Starbucks in West valley, a suburban area of Los Angeles, not far from where we both lived. I would learn that the last time that Tommy saw me I was two years old. Now at 37, with my own record label, I would also learn that was something the two of us had in common.

He told me that he had started a record label when he was 23. And in the midst of its rise, he was arrested as being one of the largest drug Kingpins in America and sentenced to life without the possibility of parole, which is death by incarceration. The government didn't want him to enjoy a life in freedom ever again and he hadn't murdered anyone.

In prison, he re-created himself into a best-selling author and a jailhouse lawyer. Around his tenth year in prison, when the money dried up and all the high-priced lawyer retreating with it, he began filing his own motion to get released. And after 25 long years he prevailed, free to start his life all over.

Our love for entertainment was what we began to build our relationship around. And I could tell right from the start that whatever assistance his friend's son needed to succeed, he was willing to help me get it. The two of us began working on all sorts of different entertainment projects, including my dad's story, "Boss Hustla," as well as this book.

It's so amazing how life works. One day, I had no idea that this man even existed and the next he's an integral part of my life.

Some days, while we are talking, I can envision the depth of the conversations he and my father must have had. And there is absolutely no subject matter about the entertainment business that my Uncle Tommy doesn't have immense knowledge about. He contributes his knowledge to having great mentors like Al Bell, the innovator of Stax Records and Forest Hamilton, the ultimate artist manager, from the Pointer Sisters to the Gap Band to Cameo.

And on other days, while we're talking, it seems as though he is speaking to me as he would a dear friend or like he would to my dad. And I recognize the place this man holds my father in his heart, and how he is now transferring that great love and respect to me.

Uncle Tommy and other men like him, helped me to realize how prison robbed me and others in my generation of valuable information. With their needed guidance and encouragement, the next generation could have successfully navigated to Black Excellence, decades before it actually began to happen.

Some might say that since they were drug dealers, they had nothing valuable to offer. Really? To those critics I would say, take a good look at our government officials. And ask yourself how so many drugs were able to reach our shores from thousands of miles away when these young black men didn't have the wherewithal: planes, boats, ships, to traffic drugs from Colombia and other cocaine producing countries. These home-grown dealers were distributing the drugs made available to them on U.S. soil, the government's dope.

These men didn't create drugs nor were they the first people to sell them. And although they sold it, they didn't force anyone to buy drugs from them. So many other races of people have sold drugs and become extremely wealthy but when black men attempted it, they were punished severely. For a nonviolent crime, they were sentenced to the harshest sentences in the history of the United States. Many of them were sentenced to death by incarceration, life sentences without the possibility of parole, which meant they would never have the opportunity to be free again. No man should have to live with that fate unless he has taken the life of another. Just imagine how that kind of pressure could affect a mind. But many of these men stood tall in their resolve, and eventually were freed after decades of imprisonment.

When history records this era, historians would be remiss not to include how absurdly ridiculous a life sentence without the possibility of parole is for a nonviolent drug crime. Especially, when people that commit murder get a shorter sentence than a person that violates U.S. drug laws. Some drug dealers still reside in a prison cell, some are even rotting away for the distribution of marijuana, a widely consumed product that has been legalized by over half of the states in the union.

During my interview of Tommy for his contribution to my dad's story, I got a sincere sense of how much he not only loved and respected my father, but also my Uncle Mike. He paid great homage to them both for giving him the opportunity to enjoy experiences that he probably wouldn't have had if he hadn't known them.

Tommy chuckled when he said, "They gave me my first opportunity to taste richness. Dave literally gave me the shirt off of his back. And with us, being around the same size, his shirts fit me well. You would only have to meet Ms. Fannie Jordan to know where he got his caring and giving personality. She was a compassionate soul to everyone around her. But if she considered you family, she would give you her last. I could never pay for a meal at her restaurant, even after I had money to pay."

By the time of this interview, Uncle Tommy had been home for six years after doing 25 years of the sentence the government had given him to die in prison. Soon after his release, he created Epi Books, which is the home of his two best sellers: American Prisoner and Star Rising. In total, he has published 12 books. He also owns TomKen Productions, a film production company, which has American Prisoner, the TV series, in development.

He told me he was the oldest child of a big family and he admired how my Uncle Michael played the excellent role of big brother taking charge of the family's well-being, essentially having the responsibility of being the head of their household, and Dave was a great younger brother. Although he didn't follow completely in Michael's steps, he was smart enough to know when Michael had come upon something that was beneficial for the both of them.

As I've come to understand, the small Louisiana town of Oak Grove, with a population two thousand souls, was where my father got much of his early training from Big Mama. And in those environs, he and Tommy met as young boys searching for their way in life.

David and Tommy, two young men with a taste for adventure and a knack for attracting women, met in that dusty little town around eleven years old. Fate had it that our cousin Willie and Tommy were friends, the bridge that connected their lives. With their shared good looks and a mutual interest in chasing skirts, the two boys hit it off immediately.

Their bond would grow stronger over the years, and whenever Tommy visited his family in Los Angeles, my dad would be the one to pick him up. They were partners in crime, always seeking excitement and thrills.

Tommy recounted a story where they were headed to a party in the hills. As they cruised along the city streets, their laughter filling the car, the flashing lights of a police car jolted them from their carefree state. The officers pulled them over, their stern voices demanding compliance. Tommy and David found themselves face down on the concrete sidewalk, their clothes dirtied by the nasty pavement. The party they were so eager to attend came to an abrupt end, their anticipation replaced by the harsh reality of the moment.

Years passed, and Tommy found himself in college, showcasing his talents on the football field. It was the spring of 1982 when dad paid him a visit, eager to support his friend.

Tommy depicted the story for me. "I walked out to the stadium's parking lot after the game and Dave was standing beside a brand-new purple Cadillac, a symbol of his success. The boy that I had become friends with at eleven years old, now a man and driving a status symbol that was more luxurious than the richest white man's car in the area.

Riding with Dave was an experience like no other. He had an infectious energy that made every moment unforgettable. It was as if I was riding with a celebrity, and Dave soaked up the attention, waving and smiling at people along the street.

We went to eat at a local restaurant, indulging in delicious Southern cuisine, a meal that was definitely too rich for my budget. During dinner, David revealed a secret, one that changed the course of my life.

Dave was excited about his new status. He told me that he was making plenty of money selling cocaine in Los Angeles. He invited me out for the summer to have a good time with him and his newfound wealth. He told me that he was flying back to LA in a few days and he was leaving his car with Willie and I should ride back with him. Willie was my dude, so that was an easy call. Then he surprised me with a wad of money.

"What's this?"

"Something to help you out for the rest of the semester."

"As we cruised around campus, Dave's car turned heads wherever we went. And Dave wasn't shy about letting willing college girls take a ride in his car. Nor was he was shy in telling them what he desired. A couple of those women asked me about Dave, long after he had flown back to LA.

The semester ended, and I jumped in my car, pointing it toward Oak Grove. I found Willie and told him my plans. He was pleased to have me join him.

A few days later, Willie and I set out, leaving the small town behind. At the time, I really didn't know it was forever. Somewhere in Texas, Willie pulled the Cadillac to the side of the highway, declaring how tired he was.

I was a team player so I had no problem with jumping behind the wheel, and navigating us for the next fourteen hours to the shorelines of San Diego. I was so young and excited that I didn't even need any sleep. With the windows down and the wind blowing, we drove along the breathtaking shoreline, the waves crashing against the sandy beaches, the salty air filling my lungs, rejuvenating my spirit.

As we were approaching Los Angeles, the city skyline came into view, and it felt magical. Of course, I had no idea that I was on an adventure that would play out in all sorts of scenarios. The bustling streets was a stark contrast to the tranquility of the countryside.

After a few days of hanging out, Dave was spending all sorts of money on me, even bought me a few outfits to go to the club in. My pride wouldn't allow me to continue taking hand-outs.

And after getting a glimpse of their operation, I decided to sacrifice whatever career I might have had in football, the allure of quick money had snared me. When I told Dave my plans, he disagreed with them, saying, I thought I would be watching you playing in the pros soon.

After seeing them making loads of money, how could I go back to school? I wouldn't have been able to focus in the classroom nor on the football field, knowing my friend was making that type of money and all I had to do was ask and I could be too.

But David urged me not to get involved. He knew the risks and the consequences that came with such a dangerous trade. I had to make a choice, one that would shape my destiny. When I told Dave that I wanted in, he washed his hands of making this decision and told me to check with Mike. Mike welcomed me into their circle, and the next day, I was working inside of a rock spot.

In a matter of months, I had quickly rose through the ranks. Willing to take on any hostile challenges for my new family, made me well-loved by all. The adrenaline rush I got when I was whipping someone's ass was similar to the ones I would get right before a big game. And eventually, Dave shook the feeling of being worried for me, especially after he witnessed the intensity of my aggression against a foe.

We all reveled in the good times, the laughter, and the camaraderie that only true friends could share. Mike and I would eventually find ourselves in the midst of a solid brotherhood, bound by our determination to become super rich.

The combined strengths of our crew made us a dynamic force, and it wasn't long before my name was ringing right alongside theirs. The dynamics of the three of us would form an allegiance that ruled LA's criminal underworld for years. The bond we forged was unwavering, as we pursued life's highest pleasures.

Dave and I would take on other drug crews in two-on-two basketball, the prize, fifty thousand dollars. Dave had lost plenty already with Deucy as his teammate. But now, we went about getting it all back. We were both around 6' 2'' and we both shot and rebounded the ball well. No crew in the city had two players that could match us.

We had front row seats at Laker games. We were invited to Magic Johnson's mid-summer night, an exhibition basketball game in the summer. We would leave the game to go to the after party at Prince's 20/20 club in Century City with all the players.

We were in LA, our town, so Dave and I were more popular with the women than superstar basketball players. And the women probably suspected that we had as much or more money than the ball players.

Michael Jordan came over and struck up a conversation, and it was obvious that he was wondering who we were. It baffled him that we were getting the attention that he was used to getting in most rooms he was present in throughout the world. Of course, we just told him our usual businessmen story.

Dave and I, not only shared a deep friendship, but also a passion for two things: horseback riding and the allure of beautiful women. Both of our body counts increased each day.

These shared interests were a source of joy, offering an escape from the complexities of our secret life, especially horseback riding. On many Sundays, David and I would saddle up our horses and gallop through the open meadows in Canyon Country, a simple joy that brought so much happiness.

The rhythmic movement of the horse beneath made me feel like a real cowboy as I rode through the untouched beauty of nature. Once we made it to a wide-open space, we would urged our horses to gallop. I would push mine as fast as she could go, the wind against my face, giving me a sense of freedom, complete and utter freedom from all that binds.

We would ride for hours on end, our laughter echoing through the countryside, providing a temporary recess from the pressures that weighed us down on most days. We loved horseback riding so much that we even invited our girlfriends to join us on a Sunday ride right after brunch."

When Uncle Tommy finished telling me about their horseback riding, I remembered seeing pictures of their outing in my mom's photo album. They all were wearing these huge smiles as they were walking toward the corral.

Tommy continued. "I hadn't realized how much charm and good looks I had until I had money. Women seemed to be attracted wherever I went, and I reveled in the excitement of flirtation and romance. When I was with Dave, I would often find myself in the company of stunning women. It was something about the laughter of women that was so inspiring. These weren't college girls but grown 21-year-old women and their conversations filled the air with a magnetic energy.

But at some point, I think we both realized that our lives were more than just fleeting moments of passion and as we recognized the importance of raising a family. And as young men, we strived to balance our desires with a sense of responsibility.

And we all knew that true success was in pursuing legitimate endeavors that would bring lasting fulfillment, especially Mike. He was always eagerly moving us into some sort of legitimate business. Not always profitable but they served as a front of legitimacy.

As we chased after our dreams, we knew there had to be more to life than the dangerous game we were playing. And we were very cognizant of our choices and that those choices could lead to incarceration. But poverty can be the catalyst for all sorts of wrong choices."

Uncle Tommy laughed when he said, "You know a brother has become very successful when he starts buying dogs. Dave owned a Chinese breed dog, a big ole furry Chow Chow with a champion bloodline that cost him two-thousand-dollars. Only a few thousand of these dogs were registered in the United States."

Uncle Tommy had intricate details about my father's life that I don't think anyone else would had, except my uncle Mike, and even then, my father and Tommy shared their own special moments that only belonged to them. Deep secrets that only the two of them shared, secrets that my father had already taken with him to his grave and as I know will go with Tommy to his grave. Because of his oath of silence, he wouldn't even share these secrets with me.

Knowing the closeness these men shared, I feel like I have a great part of my father still here with Uncle Tommy by my side, which I am immensely grateful for. Uncle Tommy will always hold a special place in my heart.

But Uncle Tommy did share with me how the name Kartier Boys kind of just stuck to them. One of their legitimate businesses was Kartier Limousine company. Uncle Mike had named it that, spelling it the same way as Cartier, the famous watch company, did. Cartier would issue and cease and desist to stop them from using their name, and Uncle Mike renamed it, changing the C to a K, Kartier. He created a jingle Kartier with a K that played on every radio station in the city.

That name got cemented after a huge fight took place at a black-tie affair. Tammy Chase, one of the baller girls, which meant she was involved in this illicit world in some way, would be the host of this party. And on the placard for their crew, she put Kartier Boys.

A few months prior, a guy in their group had been shot at because a guy from another clique thought he was messing around with his girlfriend. The guys hadn't seen the shooter and his group since that occurrence. And of all nights, they would be inside the party and sitting at the Kartier Boys table. I don't know if this was intentional but Lil Mike the guy shot at was ready to avenge the attempt on his life.

The rest of the fellows hadn't arrived. Only he and Uncle Tommy were at the party, but Lil Mike didn't care, he wanted vengeance and he wanted it immediately. Tommy tried to calm him down, to no avail. So, as a good soldier does, he accompanied his brother. When they were approaching the table, as soon as the assailant saw Lil Mike, he was quickly to his feet. Uncle Tommy snatched him by his collar, lifting him from the floor and slammed him over a table.

The rest of the assailant clique came to aid and assist him. Uncle Tommy and Lil Mike were outnumbered by 4 to 1, catching blows from every angle. The two of them fought them off as best as they could as Tommy punched his way through the crowd. Girls got in front of Lil Mike to stop the onslaught.

Tommy, seeing his brother was safe for the moment, dashed to the limo he arrived in and retrieved two nine-millimeters and rushed back into the party. Whereby, he put the whole party under arrest, and told Lil Mike to attack his assailant. Lil Mike went to work. But the other guy outweighed him by twenty pounds, and kept getting the best of Lil Mike until Uncle Tommy whacked him across the head with his pistol. A few men from the assailant's group tried to advance, and was met with the barrels of Tommy's pistol, stopping them dead in their tracks.

By the time, my dad, Uncle Mike and the rest of their crew arrived, the party was over. From that night, they were called the Kartier Boys. And there was no denying that the Kartier Boys was a known factor.

Uncle Tommy would admit that they had the wrong product in their distribution chain. He said that my dad, my uncle and he would discover that they were all ultimate salesmen, each with his own unique style. "We could sell snow to an Eskimo. T-shirts could have been our product and we still would have gotten rich. But your dad had a charm that allowed him to sell anything to anyone. He could sell air. Corporations pay for the type of talent he had.

The suddenness of his departure left us grappling with the unfairness of fate. We had weathered life's storms together, defeating poverty, celebrating victories and then he was no more. His absence left an emptiness that time can never fully heal."

ROCK HOUSE

In the lovely city of Los Angeles, amidst the glitz and glamour that adorned its surface, there existed a darker underbelly. The early 1980's was a time when law enforcement might have thought a bustling apartment complex with people going and coming meant someone was having a party, not knowing that someone had opened a rock house, a retail location that sold cocaine.

These Rock Houses were characterized by their secretive nature, often hidden in plain sight within residential areas. The houses became notorious for their constant flow of customers, as crack addiction rapidly spread throughout the city. These dens were cocaine supermarkets.

They often operated with a well-organized system, round-the-clock shifts, ensuring a steady supply of the drug. Dealers made millions of dollars off of people addicted to the drug, their customers.

Los Angeles dealers had been capitalizing on the high demand for crack cocaine for months, making millions of dollars by exploiting the addiction and vulnerability of their customers, before law enforcement began to even understand what was happening.

Among the droves of users were famous athletes and entertainers. For athletes and entertainers, smoking was more for pleasure than an escape. They could afford as much of the high as they wanted, many of them being regular shoppers.

After these little nests were eventually identified as drug operations by extensive investigation or a snitch, the latter more prevalent, it wasn't long before that location was being busted, the door kicked in and men arrested. The young men of this trade weren't deterred, opening up another spot within a few hours and fueling it with more drugs and new workers.

Raids and arrests became a common practice, but the lucrative profits associated with the drug trade made it difficult to completely eradicate the problem. The constant flow of money ensured that new dealers would quickly fill any void left by those who were apprehended.

Early on, men felt comfortable lounging or sleeping inside of these locations. They even partied inside these spots, but when the raids started, these houses were barred up like a fortress for the dealer's safety, fortifying them against police raids and robbers.

I heard that once my dad and uncle's spot was busted on Wall Street, and they just moved across King to the other side of Wall Street. They even doubled-down, opening another spot on Vernon Avenue near Alameda.

Through word of mouth, the people that had become like zombies would flock to the new location. Some of these people were once respectful citizens but after one blast (toke), of this potent drug, some users couldn't stop, the initial rush of that first blast was a gateway into a never-ending quest for the next high They would be back and forth from someone's spot all day and all night, which by this time were like liquor stores, one on every corner.

The allure of crack cocaine gripped its victims with a merciless intensity – lives forever altered, trapped in a vicious cycle of addiction. Some users became slaves to the drug's seductive power, their lives consumed by an urgent hunger that knew no bounds. Day and night, they would chase the elusive euphoria that crack offered.

But as the addiction tightened its grip, the financial toll became impossible to ignore. The middle-class and impoverished residents of Los Angeles found themselves caught in a relentless cycle of spending and depletion. In a matter of minutes, their hard-earned weekly checks, often meager to begin with, were evaporated into thin air.

A few hundred dollars that was meant to sustain them and their families would vanish quickly. The conscquences became dire, as addicts would later struggle to put food on the table or pay their bills. The desperation grcw palpable, casting a shadow over the lives of those caught in this vicious cycle.

In their despair, some women found themselves forced to make unimaginable choices. With their money gone, they would do anything to feed their unquenchable craving for crack. Selling their bodies became a means to an end. This type of woman became known as a "Strawberry," a term that carried the weight of shattered dreams and sacrificed dignity.

A Strawberry would auction off her body, forsaking her self-worth and integrity, all for just one more hit. The drug had stripped away their sense of identity, reducing her to a mere commodity in the eyes of willing dealers. The pain of her actions was buried beneath the numbing effects of crack, an escape from the harsh reality that had swallowed her whole.

And the devastation of addiction did not discriminate based on gender alone. Men, too, fell prey to the seduction of crack's embrace. They became the male counterparts to the Strawberry, known as a "Clucker." Their lives, once filled with aspirations and dreams, were reduced to hollow shells of their former selves. They, too, would sacrifice their dignity, forsaking their moral compass in pursuit of the next fix.

The ugliest part of this scene were the innocence of children that became collateral damage. The desperate cries of these young souls echoed through the night, their futures stolen away by the grasp of addiction. Mothers, once the nurturers and protectors, would sell their own flesh and blood for the promise of temporary relief. The concept of motherly love was shattered, replaced by the all-consuming cravings that knew no limitation nor end.

Shadows of desperation echoed as addicts roamed through the night in search of a way to get to their next high, in search where they lost their lives. The freaks would come out at night and they would be prowling to catch anyone slipping, ready to leap at the opportunity to take what belonged to someone else. Cars were broken into, the radios ripped from the dash, stores and people were robbed, along with a combination of many other petty crimes, so an addict could have money to buy their beloved drug.

The streets, once vibrant and teeming with life, now bore the weight of broken dreams and shattered lives. It was a city caught in the clutches of addiction, where the Strawberry and the Clucker were tragic symbols of a society in crisis.

By the middle 80s, the crack epidemic and the prevalence of rock houses became a focal point for policymakers, community leaders, and activists. Efforts were made to address the root causes of addiction, provide support and rehabilitation services for users, and implement strategies to disrupt the drug trade.

Raids and arrests were common, but the lucrative profits associated with this drug trade made it difficult to completely eradicate the problem. The constant flow of money ensured that new dealers would quickly fill any void left by those who were apprehended.

The impact of crack houses extended beyond the immediate drug trade. Communities surrounding these spots suffered from increased crime rates, including robberies, assaults, and other drug-related offenses. The presence of crack houses contributed to a sense of instability, as residents feared the consequences of addiction and the accompanying violence, leaving far-reaching and devastating impact on their community.

The operations within these crack houses were marked by a sense of danger as they began to attract not only addicted individuals seeking their next fix but also criminal elements looking to rob those that were profiting from the illicit drug trade.

This led to frequent clashes between dealers and "Jackers" (robbers) and even among rival dealers, increasing the overall level of violence in affected communities. Law enforcement agencics faced significant challenges in combating the crack epidemic and shutting down these crack houses.

In these gritty unforgiving streets, the Kartier Boys found themselves yet again facing dire circumstances. The constant threat of imprisonment loomed over them. But these individuals were not content on just accepting this fate. With unwavering determination, they harnessed their resilience to defy their circumstances and rise above the challenges they faced. Uncle Mike was wrestling with the decision to move their crack house to another area, refusing to return to poverty's clutches.

These men were more than just a group; they were a brotherhood. This group was born out of the poverty, violence, and limited resources that challenged their daily existence. They had succumb to the allure of quick money to change their dire circumstances. Men bound by shared experiences and a desire for a better life, they found strength in each other's support.

Growing up in poverty-stricken neighborhoods, they witnessed the devastating effects of limited opportunities and systemic injustices. Determined to break the cycle, they united, drawing on their collective resilience to overcome the obstacles that stood in their way and the unwavering belief that they deserved more became their marching orders. Their structure was tight, each pulling his own weight for the betterment of the whole.

But the streets that the Kartier Boys called home were tightening around their necks like a noose. Refusing to be confined by their circumstances, they made a daring decision. It was a calculated risk, but one they were willing to take to escape the clutches of the constant threat of imprisonment, and they decided to relocate their rock house to another area.

Moving was no easy feat. They faced numerous challenges along the way, including threats from rival gangs, increased law enforcement attention, and the need to establish themselves in an unfamiliar territory.

However, their resilience proved unyielding. They maneuvered these obstacles with strategic thinking, adaptability, and a deep bond that fortified their resolve. Their unwavering determination to break free from poverty drove them to push past each hurdle they encountered.

The men knew that their decision to relocate their crack houses was a necessity for survival. Their actions were playing loudly in the ears of law enforcement, so to prevent being locked away in a cage, they understood that they needed to move their operations to another jurisdiction. By moving to another area of the city could help them to evade police that knew them by name.

But regardless of how many police were dogging them, by this point, nothing would interrupt their quest to disrupt the cycle of poverty in their lives, not even the threat of prison.

SPLINTER GROUPS

The drug game was played by its own set of rules in the shadowy underworld of LA. Dealers, smugglers, and criminals of various ranks began to understand the importance of setting up buffers and insulating themselves from the ever-looming threat of prosecution. It was a survival tactic, an unwritten law that everyone beneath them on the food chain comprehended all too well. After all, if the captain of the ship went down, the whole ship would inevitably sink.

At the heart of these criminal enterprises were the bosses, captains or leaders, individuals who held the coveted position of ultimate power within the organization. They were the ones with the direct connection to a constant supply channel, the lifeblood that fueled the entire operation. These captains were gatekeepers, and their position was both envied and feared by those beneath them.

As months turned into years, soldiers lower on the food chain began to grasp the dynamics of this dicey world. Some sought to rise through the ranks, employing ruthless tactics and leveraging their skills to muscle their way to the top. Others, however, were fortunate enough to stumble upon an opportunity that would change their fortunes forever – a chance to secure their own supplier.

When a soldier managed to establish a direct connection with a supplier, a seismic shift occurred. The soldier's newfound authority sometimes disrupted the established hierarchy, challenging the captain's monopoly over the supply chain. It was at this critical juncture that one of two outcomes would unfold.

In some instances, a splinter group would take shape – a faction born out of dissent and fueled by the ambition and greed of those who craved more power and control. Dissention often happened within the ranks when soldiers didn't respect their leader. As the splinter group sought to carve out its own territory, often in direct conflict with the parent organization, men were left in difficult situations. The captain, now faced with an internal threat, had a choice to make, either defend his position, employing every resource at his disposal to maintain control and quell the uprising, or simply let it go.

Most times, the soldier who had secured his own supplier had already decided on a different path, regardless of the consequences. He would rather die than stay under the thumb of a leader that he didn't respect. In this scenario, a whole new criminal enterprise would spring forth, with the soldier as its leader. The birth of a new organization meant fresh opportunities, untapped markets, and a chance for the soldier to shape his criminal empire according to his own vision.

Many battles were started over soil that neither faction owned. Law enforcement would eventually win this war, hauling all members that weren't killed by the other faction, off to prison.

The rise of new criminal organizations became a recurring theme in this clandestine world. It was a natural consequence of the constant struggle for power, territory, and control. The criminal landscape was ever-evolving, with players constantly adapting and maneuvering to secure their place in the hierarchy.

In this perilous game, loyalties were fleeting, alliances were like eggshells, and betrayal was an ever-present threat. The bosses, aware of the shifting dynamics, became more vigilant, protecting their positions with unwavering determination. They understood that survival depended on their ability to adapt, outmaneuver, and, if necessary, eliminate any threat that dared challenge their supremacy.

In a world where the line between trust and treachery blur, and where ambition could lead to both glory and ruin, the rise of splinter groups were inevitable. Men in this life, relentlessly pursued the honor that came with power.

Out of these circumstances, men emerged like hungry predators, driven by a thirst for power and the desire to break free from the shackles of the parent organization. These renegade factions were led by soldiers who had grown tired of serving in the shadows, yearning for the spotlight of their own criminal empire.

The criminal underworld was already a labyrinth of shifting allegiances, strategic alliances, and violent clashes, bosses fighting to maintain their dominance over some of these groups. Groups that were now fueled by their newfound autonomy and thirst for power, and they began to set their sights on expanding their territories.

The new groups engaged in fierce competition with both the parent organization, other pre-existing organizations, and other upstart groups, vying for control of lucrative markets and resources. The streets became battlegrounds, where violence and bloodshed were commonplace, and survival was a constant struggle.

Some of these groups proved to be short-lived, unable to withstand the relentless pressure from rival organizations and the unyielding grip of law enforcement. They crumbled under the weight of their own ambitions, their dreams of grandeur shattered by the harsh realities of the criminal underworld.

But a select few managed to thrive, their leaders shrewd and cunning, their operations hidden within the intricate web of the criminal landscape. These groups, driven by a shared purpose and unrelenting determination, gained a foothold in the illicit trade, carving out their own domains and establishing a reputation for themselves.

As more and more groups entered the playing field, the criminal underworld became pieces of the power struggle puzzle as numerous other factions, each with its own chain of command, supply channels, and code of conduct, emerged. Loyalties shifted, alliances formed and dissolved, and the balance of power continuously teetered on a knife's edge.

Law enforcement agencies, overwhelmed by the sheer magnitude of criminal activity, struggled to keep pace with the ever-evolving landscape. While they aimed to dismantle the entire network, their focus shifted to disrupting and dismantling one organization at a time. As they targeted the leaders, new figures rose to take their place, ensuring the survival and continuity of the criminal enterprises.

Some of these new groups, though smaller in scale, proved to be nimble, adaptable, and elusive, intensifying the competition within the criminal underworld but this also presented new opportunities for those willing to exploit the chaos. The groups operated in the same shadows, leveraging their intimate knowledge of their prior group to dominate them while leveraging their knowledge of the criminal underworld to evade capture and maintain a steady flow of illicit goods.

Some groups that split became more powerful than the original group, waging a silent war against the parent organizations, employing every tactic at their disposal to seize control of lucrative territories and establish their dominance. They struck at the heart of their former comrades, exploiting weaknesses and vulnerabilities, and leaving a trail of chaos and destruction in their wake.

Independent players, bankers, entrepreneurs, and opportunists entered the fray, seeking to form alliances or exploit the vulnerabilities of the fragmented landscape and stake a claim to a portion of the treasure trove of wealth. It was a time of uncertainty, where fortunes rose and fell, and the line between success and failure blurred.

In this ever-shifting underworld, power was transient, and survival depended on one's ability to adapt and seize opportunities. The leaders, once untouchable in their positions of authority, now faced the constant threat of being dethroned by their own soldiers or rival factions. Many criminal empires, that were once a monolithic entity, had fractured into a myriad of factions, some interconnected but other autonomous entities, each vying for supremacy.

In these dimly lit corridors, treachery lurked like a venomous serpent. The rise of separate groups painted a picture of ambition, rivalry, and the ever-present shadows of betrayal. Men who dared to challenge the status quo, men ever eager to climb the ladder of influence, eyed their leaders with a mixture of admiration and envy. They yearned for the day when they could ascend to the coveted position of power, where the spoils of the illicit trade would be theirs to command. The game of power had turned into a ruthless dance, where alliances were made and broken with the flick of a light – loyalty a feeble illusion.

But as the soldiers carved their way through the ranks, their eyes fixed on the ultimate prize, the allure of personal gain began to overshadow the notion of loyalty. Greed whispered its seductive promises, beckoning them to abandon the very foundations that had once bound them to their comrades. It was in this cauldron of ambition that the seeds of betrayal took root.

Under the guise of camaraderie and brotherhood, soldiers maneuvered with calculated precision, seeking to secure their own supply channels and establish their reign. They weaved intricate webs of deceit, playing both sides of this vicious game, all while keeping a watchful eye on their fellow soldiers.

The whispers of discontent grew louder within the ranks, like a poison spreading through the veins of the organization. The soldiers who had managed to secure their own suppliers now found themselves at the center of a delicate balancing act. They had become the new captains, and with that title came the burden of maintaining their authority.

But amidst this brutal power struggle, loyalty became a scarce commodity. Betrayal, like a venomous snake, slithered through the ranks, striking when least expected.

A bigger problem became apparent. Men that had splintered from their commitment to their organization. Soldiers turned informants, sharing vital information with law enforcement agencies in exchange for their own safety and immunity. The once impenetrable fortress of the criminal underworld was now riddled with cracks, leaking secrets that threatened to bring the entire edifice crashing down.

This treacherous game unfolded behind prison walls. Men who had once stood shoulder to shoulder, their brotherhood forged in the crucible of illicit endeavors, now found themselves torn apart by the bitter sting of betrayal.

When the handcuffs tightened around their wrists and the cold steel bars slammed shut, desperation set in. Faced with the prospect of a lengthy sentence, some men chose a path paved with treachery. They became snitches, transforming from trusted confidants to undercover informants, their allegiance shifting from brotherhood to self-preservation.

With whispers exchanged in dimly lit cells and secret meetings in hidden corners, these snitches embarked on a perilous mission. They began assisting law enforcement, providing crucial information to bring down those they had once called their brothers. No stone was left unturned in their pursuit to escape the confines of a prison, even if it meant tearing apart the very fabric of loyalty that had once bound them together.

The snitch's heart raced as they walked the tightrope between two worlds. Each interaction with law enforcement carried the weight of a double-edged sword, balancing on a precarious precipice of danger and deceit. They risked their lives, forever marked as traitors, haunted by the shadows of their past choices.

For some, the motivation to snitch stemmed from a desire for redemption, a chance to right the wrongs they had partaken in. But for others, self-preservation was the driving force, a desperate bid to secure a lighter sentence or escape the clutches of a life behind bars. In their pursuit of freedom, they willingly cast aside their moral compass, leaving a trail of shattered trust in their wake.

The consequences of their actions reverberated through the underworld. Arrests were made, once impenetrable criminal networks dismantled piece by piece. The snitch's role became a catalyst for change, a betrayal that sent shockwaves through the ranks of organized crime. The lines between friend and foe blurred, as paranoia gripped those who had managed to evade capture.

The life of a snitch was far from glamorous. They lived in constant fear, forever marked as a target for retribution. The consequences of their actions were twofold, as they faced the wrath of both law enforcement and the criminal underworld. Betrayal was a double-edged sword, cutting deep into their souls.

In the twisted realm of crime and loyalty, the snitch became a tragic figure. They were trapped between their past and their present, haunted by the choices that had forever altered their lives. The scars of their betrayal ran deep, a constant reminder of the price they had paid for their survival.

The delicate threads that held criminal brotherhoods together didn't prove strong enough to withstand the strain of wanting more, needing more. Trust was a rare and precious commodity, easily shattered but difficult to rebuild. Even the strongest bonds could be broken by the allure of self-preservation.

The leaders, aware of the ever-present danger, tightened their grip on power, employing ruthless tactics to weed out traitors within their ranks.

Paranoia became their constant companion, as they questioned the loyalty of even their most trusted allies. The once unbreakable bonds of brotherhood were shattered, replaced by a climate of suspicion and fear.

In this turbulent landscape, survival meant adapting to the ever-changing dynamics of the underworld. The players danced a dangerous tango of deception, manipulation, and violence. They handled uncertain waters, forever aware that betrayal could come from within their own ranks to clench them around their throat when they were least expecting it.

Other organizations and groups weaknesses, were the Kartier Boys' strengths. Their top brass were kindred spirits with one sole purpose, escaping poverty, and they were all united under one flag, the Money flag.

STEVIE

If you have ever wondered why a rapper has a few different handles, you have to look no further than the history of the boys in the hood. The men called "go-getters" will be known by several nicknames, some depending on attributes like Black or Big but others were created because of other attributes like acting like a dog or a man could be nicknamed "Killer" because of the number of people they have killed. Rappers, mimicking their street heroes, call themselves some of these names without having hoodlum deeds nor any street creds whatsoever.

Steve "Whitey" Robinson, whom I affectionately call Uncle Whitey, is a man that has earned the right to be called a boss. When I officially met him, he struck me as somewhat of a hood historian. I know his book, LA Chronicles, will be a phenomenal read.

Having lived a criminal lifestyle since he was twelve, he knew all the top players from his era in every hood, which was well into the thousands. Uncle Whitey was very instrumental as a source of so much valuable information for this book.

I met him at his restaurant, Just Poppin, on 25th and Central for this interview. He is still very involved with the community he grew up in. He does an annual party for Juneteenth as well as the 4th of July. My music company, Blank Kanvas, provided the entertainment for his Juneteenth Block Party 2023.

I would learn that Whitey personally commanded hundreds of troops called Whitey Enterprise, a clique within the Broadway gang. When Whitey showed up at an event or a hang out, he would have dozens of soldiers with him. As we were talking, I knew I was in the presence of greatness. It was as if I was sitting with a general.

From having my ear to the streets, I knew that Whitey's voice was still heard as one that the streets of LA listened to, a voice that demanded a great deal of respect, even from men in my generation.

Uncle Whitey told me that he and my dad were like brothers. "By the time I was around fifteen, I was a force to be reckoned with in the world of illicit enterprises. From a young age, I had an uncanny knack for maneuvering in these streets and building connections. It was during our formative years that fate brought me face to face with another young hustler by the name of David "Black Dave" Harris."

Whitey told me that the force he commanded was available any time that my dad needed it but fortunately he never did, at least not to subject bodily harm against another. But he did use it as a show of force once and after that night, the city knew the two groups were allied. With the city being put on notice, those that may have thought of trying to do something foolish, forgot about it.

"The city knew my guys were allies with Mike and Dave. It was a dozen or so of them in their crew, making them as big as any clique in any LA gang. And they had their own men who would avenge any disrespect (hitters), and having my guys to aid and asset them was a valuable tool. They always stuck together and that's what made them so strong. In those days, it wasn't any holes in their game, meaning they were air tight.

Your dad and I had many similarities. We both loved the conquest of beautiful women, fast toys (cars), and lots of money. I was impressed by him. And I'm rarely impressed by anyone. I feel like there is none more superior than I.

But your dad held my attention as he did the attention of countless others. Women went crazy over him when he arrived at any location as if he was as popular as your most popular movie star or recording artist.

In the tough streets of LA, your dad and I quickly established ourselves as the go-to guys for anyone seeking to score drugs on a large scale. We both possessed an entrepreneurial spirit that set us apart from our peers, and it wasn't long before everyone recognized it.

Although some people considered what we were doing as wrong, we did what we had to do to not live the nonexistent life of poverty. I didn't know any other way to get what I saw so many white people with, except rob them for it and I wasn't a natural robber. But don't get it mixed up, I will rob not to be hungry.

Mine and Dave's friendship was forged in that type of environment, where real friends are made, where loyalty is everything. We shared our dreams, ambitions, and, more importantly, our love. Dave and I were brothers in every sense of the word. We shared triumphs and setbacks, joys and sorrows. We celebrated birthdays, holidays, and milestones together, creating memories that have lasted a lifetime.

I was street-savvy, always one step ahead of the game. I had the ability to read people and situations, which made me a natural leader. My reputation and influence grew from a gang environment.

Dave came from a different background. His mother, your grandmother, Fannie, ran a café on 51st and Central, a place where all of us would get fed delicious food. She is the reason her sons understood how to hustle to get what they wanted. It was a proud day when they had made enough money to buy her the café that she once was only an employee.

Dave rarely listened to his older brother, Mike, unless he could really see a benefit in it. The men were definitely sibling rivals. But that energy was what pushed them. When one of them took a giant step, the other one replicated it.

One day, Mike bought an eighth (three grams) of cocaine and started selling in the front yard on 46th. The next day, Dave bought him one, and also started selling it on 46th. When Mike complained, Dave simply said, this is my mama's house too.

I don't want you to ever think that they didn't loved each other. They just showed their love in their own way. But I know the special bond they had for each other. Dave just had his own mind and Mike needed a younger brother he could lead and he couldn't lead Dave. So, Mike went out and found younger brothers that would allow him to lead them. And Dave basically was solo. He liked being by himself or with whatever woman he chose for the day or week or month.

And Fannie was the engine that made both men go. She had a heart of gold and treated everyone who walked through her doors like family. Fannie took a special liking to me. She became my mother as much as she was Dave's and Mike's. Dave had passed and Mike was away on vacation (prison)," Whitey said, his tone serious, "I looked after her as I did my own mother."

Whitey would tell me that his mother's house on 43rd and Avalon became a sanctuary for Dave. He was always welcome there, and Whitey's mother treated him like one of her own. The house was a reflection of Whitey's success, filled with expensive foreign cars that he had acquired through his hustling endeavors.

Whitey would chronicle for me more of their life together. "Dave would often take the keys to one of these cars, leaving the key of his car for me to drive. Our partnership grew on trust and mutual understanding. We complemented each other's strengths, my street smarts combined with Dave's analytical mind and strategic thinking created a formidable duo.

Whitey Enterprise was expanding across LA and the Kartier Boys were too, both burgeoning empires. We built a network of loyal customers and ruthless enforcers who would stop at nothing to protect our interests.

Of course, our type of lifestyle has pressures but we were the type of men that dealt with anything that came our way. Black Dave's respect level rose to such a level that there wasn't a neighborhood he wasn't welcomed in. He was one of the most trustworthy guys I have ever met. He had a Mexican plug and I've witnessed him go around town, pick up his customer's money, literally millions of dollars. And no one worried about would he return with their supply.

He was so well respected that if he ever had a problem with anyone, a number of crews were coming to aid and assist, including me and anyone that loved me or if soldiers to handle whatever kind of problem had occurred.

Usually if Dave was there, he was trying to negotiate the peace, intervening in someone else's problem. There was never an occasion that I remember someone wanted to do something harmful to him. I'm sure there were plenty guys that hated that the woman that they once dated had chosen Dave but they never voiced their anger in public nor did they let any ill feeling get back to us.

Know this one fact, if you don't already, Deucy was with Dave more than any other person. He loved Deucy, from the day he brought him to live in their house. Deucy, not only became his brother, but Mike's too. Deucy could do no wrong, and anything he needed Dave made sure he had it.

But I think when Dave stepped out on the town, Tommy would be with him or they would have arranged to be at the same location. My crew and I would show up in numbers at parties in Beverly Hills and Hollywood, and women were either chasing your dad or your Uncle

Tommy.

Black Dave and Tommy, who I call Black Tommy because as soon as he got out here from Louisiana, Dave brought him to my spot in Leimert Park. I remember the day that they came by, I had a line around the corner, selling them my G-boulders, which were huge grams of cocaine.

And I knew if Dave trusted anyone enough to bring him to my spot, he was a good dude in my book. So, from the first day I met him, he has been Black Tommy to me. Both of them had that Louisiana dark skin.

When I saw them I saw twins, twins in ambition and twins in spirit. They had a lot of similarities. They even looked alike. Both were born hustlers, and you could just see how much they both loved and admired each other.

All of the men in their crew breathed air that most people never breathed – rare air as it's called. All of them had a job to do and their combined strengths made them a force to be reckoned with in these streets.

Individually, their top guys became household names, before the streets started calling their collective group, the Kartier Boys. Dave following his brother's lead into legitimacy, opened a limousine company called Kartier Limousine, and that's where that name came from. Besides the limousine company, Dave owned a car lot in Anaheim, a car wash, and rent-a-car service.

When the money began to roll in, most of us moved our main homes away from the hood. Dave and I would often joke that we lived three freeways away from LA. Dave bought a house in Encino and Mike bought one around the corner. Your Uncle Mike was friends with Mayor Bradley. But when law enforcement discovered that they were major players in the drug game, Mayor Bradley was forced to confiscate both men's homes.

Your dad always looked the part, an impeccable dresser, well-groomed at all times, his aura next level. He was also a fearless gambler. Most people would flinch after they lost a lot of money and concede. He would lose a hundred thousand, get another hundred thousand and win three hundred thousand. He always believed that he would come out of top.

Eventually, law enforcement moved in to close down our shops, ending our brand of glory. And we would be sentenced to prison terms equivalent to a person that had committed murder. This signified to me, how seriously they wanted to stamp out our efforts to become wealthy.

As you depart from me, no matter who wants to eliminate our lifestyle, I want you to know that the tale of Black Dave has become a legend in the annals of the Low Bottoms. Your dad's memory will live on forever. And as long as I live, I can personally assure you that he will always be remembered.

A ROCK STAR WAS BORN

The ideal or quintessential representation of what it means to be a rock star is embodied in his characteristics, persona, and lifestyle. This term is usually associated with successful and iconic figures in the rock music industry. While there may be variations and individual interpretations, some common elements of the epitome of a rock star include, possessing a unique and influential style that sets them apart. A rock star commands attention with their charisma. They have a magnetic aura and the ability to energize and connect with his/her audience.

Rock stars often cultivate a distinct visual identity that becomes synonymous with their persona. This may include flamboyant or rebellious fashion choices, memorable hairstyles, or other visual elements that contribute to their overall image.

They possess an undeniable charm that draws people in. This type of star has a certain style that makes them captivating. A rock star is associated with a rebellious, free-spirited, and non-conformist attitude. They are often seen as rule-breakers, risk-takers, and trendsetters who challenge societal norms and embrace a hedonistic lifestyle.

Rock stars have a dedicated and passionate fan base that idolizes and supports them. Their energy resonates deeply with their audience and inspires a sense of loyalty and devotion. The epitome of a rock star is that he or she leaves a lasting impact, creating a craze that influences future generations and shapes evolution. Their legacy extends beyond their own life, inspiring aspiring followers and leaving an indelible mark on the world.

According this definition, Dave had successfully turned the corner from ordinary to amazing. From every corner of the city, his name was being yelled. For whatever a reason a person's popularity grows, his had – and it translated with a lot of people.

He had been elevated to the stature of Rock Star status. By all accounts, he was hood fabulous. People idolized him. Fast cars were his favorite and women ran a close second. He was definitely a nonconformist, defying law enforcement.

It was reported that one lady once asked him, "Why don't you become a movie star."

And he responded, "The streets is all I know."

In every corner of LA as well as other cities, he was known. If people didn't know him personally, they spoke of his growing legend.

His customary dress style was slacks and a shirt with suede shoes, no socks. This outfit could cost upwards of two thousand dollars. For casual wear, he would be in the latest designer sweat suit, Fila BJ, the suit that the famous tennis player endorsed, or either he would be wearing some other designer tracksuit: Diadora, Ellesse or Sergio Tacchini. LA's warm climate allowed a person to wear this type of gear year-round, if they could afford it.

For special events like parties or concerts, he would be wearing an expensive Italian suit – Brioni, more than five thousand dollars a suit, wearing the appearance of any other famous movie star or basketball player. Around athletes and entertainers, he fit in seamlessly. Even amongst the legitimate rich and famous, he stood out in the crowd.

As we say in the hood. He stayed suited and booted. It would be fair to say that snazzy dressers in the 80's like my dad created the style for

Pop Culture then and now.

From Magic Johnson's Mid-Summer Night exhibition basketball game to Byron Scott's (Laker player) New Year's Eve party, Dave hobnobbed with the in-crowd. Any room he walked into, women's heads turned. Even with other famous men in the room, he stole the show, his good looks neutralizing their thunder.

Electrifying Power

Once one comes into themselves to the point of truly knowing who they are, confidence exudes from every fiber of their being. A person like this looks very attractive to the rest of us.

Lights, Camera, Confidence!

Imagine stepping onto a stage, the spotlight shining down on you, and a hush falling over the crowd. You take a deep breath, feeling an electrifying energy surge through your veins. What's the secret to this captivating presence? It's the power of self-discovery, the key that unlocks your inner superstar and unleashes an irresistible confidence that sets you aglow – a show-stopping magnetic force that dazzles and delights those around you.

This can be likened unto a thrilling treasure hunt. When one grabs their metaphorical shovel and start digging deep within them self, unearthing the hidden gems that make them shine, they uncover their passions, their strengths, and even those quirky little quirks that make them uniquely them.

It's an "aha" moment that leaves one initial breathless until they become accustomed. By all accounts, dad was feeling himself every single moment of every day. He knew who he was and the magnificent energy he possessed.

He had shed the disguises and masks to please others and went about each day just being himself, love him or hate him, he was Black Dave and Black Dave aimed to please Black Dave. He stepped into the spotlight, unapologetically embracing his authentic self.

This type of genuineness caused many to gasps in awe as he revealed his alluring personality. He danced to his own rhythm, singing his own song, and those around him couldn't help but be enchanted by this audacious display of realness. His was a symphony of confidence that reverberated throughout the world.

Bravo, Bravo, Bravo!

Many people that I interviewed said that dad's confidence was like a shimmering halo, illuminating his every move. Even his body language exuded a magnetic charm, his words carrying weight and conviction, and his actions spoke volumes. He walked tall, head held high, radiating an irresistible appeal. The crowd couldn't help but admire him. His confidence was mesmerizing. His fashion sense was decades ahead of the times. And his unwavering belief in himself and his ability to conquer any challenge with style and grace was intoxicating.

Rarely does an entire city stand and give a player a standing ovation. And Dave was just not a known figure in LA's underworld but in the underworld at large, and even amongst celebrities. He owned a hair salon in Hollywood where famous women and the wives of famous men frequented. It was where they would get the opportunity to witness his glamour.

His was the star that shined brightly, inspiring and uplifting those around him. He always encouraged others, to embrace their uniqueness to step into their own spotlight. Many people's inner superstars was unleashed as a result of witnessing his.

Dave was an ongoing performance, a never-ending encore that kept the audience on their feet. He would continue to evolve, to grow, and to discover new facets of himself. The spotlight followed him wherever he went.

The show must go on, and he reveled in the thrill of the unexpected, knowing that with each act, he became more extraordinary, more captivating, and more unstoppable.

His authentic personality shined like fireworks on a starry night. Not even death, can even contain his magnificence.

Cue the confetti cannons and get ready for a show-stopping conclusion!

Ladies and gentlemen give yourself a thunderous round of applause for the unstoppable confidence that comes from within you! The curtain may fall, but the show never truly ends. Embrace the encore, the never-ending applause for more of your realness. Each day is an opportunity to unveil new layers of your brilliance, to tap into undiscovered talents, and to redefine what it means to be confidently you.

So, keep the spotlight shining bright. Embrace the stage of life with all its twists, turns, and unexpected surprises. Dance through the challenges, sing your heart out with passion, and let your confidence radiate like a disco ball, lighting up every room you enter.

Encore, Encore, Encore!

His confidence was contagious, like a catchy tune that everyone wants to sing along to. The city would await with anticipation what was coming next, new car, new house, or a new fashion style. His talents were more suited for a motivational speaker because he had the ability to inspire others, encouraging them to embrace their authentic self, and to remember the power they held within their being.

I encourage everyone to go out there and shine like the superstar you are. Let the world witness your brilliance. The applause is thunderous, the cheers are deafening, and the journey ahead is nothing short of extraordinary.

The world is your stage, and you're destined to steal the show! Due to dad's untimely passing, I will make my best attempt at doing his Swan song. And I will give to the world a glimpse into the life of Black Dave in the movie, "Boss Hustla."

LARUE

"Dave was heartbroken when LaRue was killed. He called me all the time to see if LaRue Jr. and I needed anything," Aunt Yvette said as she shared memories of my dad.

"We often went out to dinner with your parents. Your mom and I shared a special bond, both pregnant women at the time. My son, LaRue Jr. is only a two-months younger than you. I remember the day you were born. LaRue and I were officially made your godparents at Smyrna Seventh Day Adventist church on Washington.

Although your mother Robin and I are lasting friends, and I have other very close friends but I don't think I've ever seen two people as close as LaRue and Dave were. They loved so many of the same things which made their relationship easy. From gambling shacks to Laker Games to Jet skiing, those men really enjoyed each other's company. I have never witnessed closer friends, nor have I seen such a true friendship since their passing.

LaRue would have a lot of his friends come over to my mom's house on 4th Avenue and there was never a dull moment. This lively atmosphere was a perfect backdrop for exciting times. Your dad had a way of standing out amongst the crowd. I think it was his easy-going style and his genuine smile that made him so special to everyone. And anything that the men were playing: dice, dominoes, cards, your dad hated to lose.

He also loved to prank, from tapping someone on the opposite shoulder to make them look in that direction to see no one there, to gently touching a sleeping person's nose with a string to cause them to attempt clearing this pest from their face. His joking displayed his jolly side. I guess men that live such a serious existence need a time to unwind. And when they were together, they could relax.

My mom loved cooking, and when LaRue told her that some of his friends would be coming over, she would always cook something. And Dave enjoyed her cooking, and after eating a big plate of food, he would find a comfortable spot on the soft cushiony couch in the living room, and fall asleep. His snores would blend with the background noise of our laughter and conversation.

It was during these visits that LaRue witnessed a side of Dave that endeared him even more to his friend. Dave's voracious appetite for more of life mirrored his own. Living life to the fullest, never holding back, was LaRue's motto, and he had found his kindred spirit in Dave and Dave in him.

Although Dave was about a foot taller than LaRue, they both had these larger than life personalities that drew people to them like a magnet. Their infectious charm and quick wit made them a favorite among friends and strangers alike. It was no surprise that they hit it off as soon as their lives crossed paths. They were kindred spirits, both with a taste for adventure and a passion for taking risks.

Black Dave, as everyone called him, was a relentless force of energy. He was always on the go, seeking out the next big bet or adventure. LaRue admired his friend's unwavering enthusiasm and often found himself caught up in Dave's whirlwind of excitement. Together, they would embark on countless escapades, seeking out unconventional bets and pushing the boundaries of their own daring. Whether it was a high-stakes dice game or a friendly wager on trivial matters, they thrived on the thrill of taking risks and testing their luck.

Their gambling adventures took them to various places: from the glittering lights of Las Vegas to underground dice games at gambling shacks in the heart of the city. They reveled in the thrill of chance, strategizing, and outsmarting opponents, always pushing each other to new heights. I never understood how they did it, but they would spend hours placing bets at a Crap table, their competitive edge ignited by the anticipation of victory. Theirs was friendship forged in the fires of danger and risks.

But it wasn't just about the money for LaRue and Dave. They both had more money than they could ever spend, especially more than that could ever be made in a Crap game. It was about their brotherhood, the shared experiences, and the unspoken understanding between them. Of course, money was the cherry on top, but for young men coming from meager beginnings and witnessing so many failures, a victory meant a lot, any kind of victory, any way they could get it.

Flying by the seat of their pants was another passion they shared. They both had a thirst for adrenaline and a desire to break free from the mundane. Whenever they had the chance, they were placing a bet, and on anything. They would bet on a cock roach race. Them and their friends would pull their cars up anywhere in Los Angeles underneath a street light in an empty parking lot and start a dice game.

Their adventures were filled with laughter, heart-pounding moments, and the unbreakable bond that comes from sharing such experiences. The two young men were partners in crime, bound by a love for the pursuit of excitement."

Showtime, Baby!

Black Dave had front-row seats at the Forum in Inglewood where the Lakers played. He would often invite a friend to watch a Laker game with him. LaRue sat in his extra seat often. They were both die-hard Lakers fan, and the energy of the crowd was what they loved even more. The love for crowd energy ran deeply in both of their veins.

Dave and LaRue found themselves in an unforgettable moment at the Forum, the Los Angeles Lakers' home during this time. As they settled into their seats, an electric atmosphere enveloped the arena. Dave's seats were close to the legendary Jack Nicholson, a staple at Lakers games. The anticipation in the air was palpable as Magic Johnson and his talented squad prepared to take on the formidable Golden State Warriors, led by the skilled shooting forward, Chris Mullin. With each possession, the crowd erupted in excitement, their eyes fixated on the court. Dave and LaRue soaked in the energy, witnessing a clash of basketball titans amidst the glitz and glamour of the Forum.

As a Warrior takes a last second shot and misses, Magic Johnson grabs the rebound, and slow rolled the ball to the other end of the court, a Warrior player chases after it as the crowd watched the clock tick to zero. Dave leaped from his court-side seat and his excited eyes were seen on the Jumbo-Tron and for the world watching on television.

We are our fathers' sons.

Growing up, I spent a lot of time with LaRue Jr. We were like brothers, bonded by the memories and stories of our fathers. We often found ourselves daydreaming about what life would have been like if we hadn't lost them before we even had a chance to even know them. We wondered how they would have shaped our lives as well as the adventures we would have gone on together.

We discussed the experiences our fathers enjoyed. La Rue would often occupy the extra Laker's season seats that my dad had. They both had their favorite players and they would cheer them, high-fiving, and engaging in animated discussions about the team's performance. The

Lakers games at the Forum became a venue where their friendship could blossom, a place where they could let loose as they indulged in their shared passion.

Along their travels, LaRue and Dave would meet Fat Dobbie while gambling one night. Men of those days would spend an additional fifty thousand dollars to accessorize a new car, from rims to kits to car stereos, to putting any of the latest top of the line accessories on their cars.

Fat Dobbie instantly became a confidant and a go-to man for automobile parts to dress up their expensive cars, even more. He knew all the spots where the fanciest adornments were sold. Or, if the men were fixing up a classic car, Dobbie would know which junk yard to visit to buy what they needed.

A few nights a week, Dave, LaRue and Dobbie would meet up at some gambling shack around the city. Dobbie differed from the two of them, only betting that the dice didn't hit, meaning whichever point the shooter was trying to make, he didn't believe he could. LaRue and Dave believed that they could hit every point if they were shooting the dice.

LaRue Sr.'s untimely demise was a tragedy that changed the course of his family's life as did my dad's accidental drowning, sending shockwaves through my family's life, through a whole community of people's lives.

LaRue Sr. was brutally taken from this world while having lunch at a restaurant. A man walked in and shot him dead right at the table. Though I didn't have the privilege of knowing him personally, the stories I've heard about him always fill me with a sense of adoration. LaRue Sr. was a man who lived life on his own terms, unafraid to take risks and embrace the unknown. I learned that he approached every day with the pleasure of living a satisfying day.

With the memories of my dad and LaRue Sr. intertwined, I found solace in the bond I shared with LaRue Jr. Together, we lived lives to honor our fathers' legacies as we forged our own paths. We supported each other through the ups and downs, drawing strength from the stories we had grown up with and the unspoken understanding that our fathers' spirits were with us every step of the way. We understood that we had a responsibility to carry on their legacies, to live lives that reflected their passion and fearlessness.

In the quiet moments of reflection, we also acknowledge the bittersweet reality that our fathers are not physically here to witness our accomplishments. But their absence serves as a constant reminder of life's brevity and the urgency to make the most of every moment we have. It fuels our determination to continue living in a way that honors their memory, cherishing the friendships we have and embracing the adventure that life has to offer as we channel their energy.

Though we may never fully know the men our fathers were, their stories and the impact they had on those around them continue to fuel our own journeys. We carry their spirits within us, drawing strength from their resilience, courage, and zest for life. They have become our guiding lights, illuminating our paths through the darkest of times and inspiring us to reach for greatness.

As we look towards the future, we know that our fathers' legacies will continue to shape our journeys. We will carry their spirits with us, seeking new adventures, embracing the unknown, and spreading their message of living life to the fullest. We will honor their memory not only through our actions but also by inspiring others to embrace their own passions, forge meaningful connections, and leave a lasting impact on the world.

As the years passed, LaRue Jr. and I found ourselves embracing our passions and living lives that echoed the adventures our fathers had once pursued. We took risks, explored new horizons, and pushed the boundaries of what we believed was possible. Through it all, we carried the memories of our fathers in our hearts, their spirits fueling our determination and reminding us of the lives they had lived.

When I look at LaRue Jr., I see the splitting image of the man that I've only seen in pictures, his dad, even down to his silky hair texture, except he's a darker version. I love that he and I had the chance to grow up together, spending our summers in Ladera Heights as youth with many of our other cousins. Ours was a natural bond, forged from the absence of our fathers, that made me feel closer to him than my real brothers at times.

Much like our fathers, we shared similar interests as young boys growing into young men. We both loved to play video games, girls, nice clothes and music. We were two kids growing up on legendary stories about our fathers. We heard stories of the things the men did when they were together and about their individual exploits. This experience made our relationship different, special! The understanding of the pride and pain we both held in our hearts, enhanced our bonding even more.

Of course, as boys growing up without our biological fathers, our journeys were filled with challenges. There were moments when self-doubt crept in, when the weight of our fathers' legacies felt heavy on our shoulders. In those moments, we leaned on each other for support, drawing strength from the unique relationship we shared. We reminded ourselves that our fathers' lives were not defined by their tragic endings but by the way they lived and the joy they brought to others.

The loss of our fathers has molded us into individuals who understand the value of time, the importance of cherishing every moment, and the significance of leaving a lasting impact. We strive not only to honor their memory but also to create a legacy of our own, one that will inspire future generations.

As I reflect on the journey that brought me to this point, I am grateful for the friendship between LaRue Sr. and my dad. Their connection not only shaped their lives but also influenced the trajectory of mine. It serves as a confirmation of the power of friendship, the bonds that transcend time, and the impact that even brief encounters can have on our lives.

Today, as I sit in my front-row seat at Lakers games, I feel a sense of fulfillment. The memories of my father and the stories that surround him flood my mind, reminding me of the unique path I have walked. The cheering crowd and the electrifying energy of the game serve as evidence of the heights that a determined person can reach.

My father left us a gift far greater than any material possession. He has given me the gift of friendship, of shared memories, and of a deep understanding of what it means to truly live.

Black Dave and LaRue Sr.'s friendship has transcended time and space, and it has become the foundation upon which I build my own life. I've delved into the world of art and entrepreneurship, and I aimed to inspire others to stay resilient and to elevate to their highest potential.

In the midst of our personal pursuits, LaRue Jr. and I never lost sight of the bond that connected us. We remained steadfast in our friendship, supporting each other through the highs and lows of life. We celebrated each other's victories and provided solace in times of sorrow. Our friendship is a constant reminder of the unbreakable link between our fathers and the legacy they left behind.

LaRue Jr. and I have come a long way since we first dreamed of the lives we could have had if our fathers were still here. We have transformed those dreams into realities, crafting lives that honor their memory and inspire others to live with passion and purpose. Our fathers' larger than life personalities continue to guide us, their spirits forever intertwined with our own.

And as we continue on our journey, we carry the torch of their friendship and the lessons learned from their tremendous drive as well as their mistakes. We embrace the unknown as we live lives that would make them proud.

In the end, LaRue Sr.'s legacy lives on through his son, LaRue Jr., and my father's through me. We carry the torch of their friendship, the spirit of adventure, and the essence of living life to the fullest. I can't help but feel a sense of gratitude for the unbreakable bond that was forged between our fathers and the enduring friendship that now lives on within us. The power of connection, the beauty of shared experiences, and the immense impact that a single friendship can have on other people's lives, are displayed in their dynamic relationship.

ROBIN

David Harris stood tall and confident, his deep brown eyes scanning the restaurant as he awaited Karen, his date. He was setting his brother Michael up with one of her friends. And David was looking forward to a fun evening on this double date.

As the door swung open, Karen walked in, accompanied by a stunning young woman. David's breath caught in his throat as he laid eyes on Karen's friend. Karen would walk over and introduce Robin to Mike and Dave.

Robin was a beautiful brown complexioned lady with a radiant smile and an infectious laugh. Her grace and elegance were captivating, and David couldn't help but feel drawn to her. He extended his hand with a warm smile. "Hey, I'm David," his voice strong and dark, titillating.

"It's a pleasure to meet you, I'm Robin. Karen has told me so much about you," Robin said, her voice filled with genuine warmth and her eyes sparkling as she shook his hand.

When they were seated at their table, David couldn't help but notice the immediate connection between them. They laughed and chatted effortlessly, their conversation flowing as if they had known each other for years. As the evening progressed, David had almost forgotten about the lady on this date with him, finding himself captivated by Robin's intelligence, kindness, and beauty.

At least that's the way I imagined it.

As I was growing into a young man, mom would tell me all sorts of tales about the legitimate businesses that my dad owned at only twenty-four years old. It wasn't until I attempted to start my own business that I understood that mom wasn't telling me the whole truth. When I questioned her, she finally came clean as she reluctantly told me that dad was really a drug kingpin. It all made sense then. Dad had jump started all the businesses he owned with drug money.

I would come to understand that my darling mother, who sacrificed her life for her children, sometimes appear to be unbelievably naïve about the goings-on in the underworld. Especially, when she said that she didn't have any idea about dad's business. A young black man driving around in a hundred and sixty thousand Ferrari, should have given her some clue.

My mom's friend, Karen, that brought her on the double date, was actually setting her up with Uncle Michael. As soon dad saw my mother, he had other plans. After the date, dad was so intrigued by mom that he pursued her and eventually won her heart. Karen's introduction became a pivotal moment that sparked a deep connection, leading to a relationship that would shape my life.

Robin Melton was one of several women competing for David's affection, and would bear him two sons. Their love story unfolded amidst the backdrop of David's dangerous lifestyle, creating a complex dynamic where Robin's devotion and their shared parenthood added both joy and vulnerability to their relationship.

Mom was the missus; the one dad had chosen to make babies with. As I've heard from so many of his friends and comrades, gangsters chose women that weren't in the streets and that had a totally opposite lifestyle from theirs to bear children for them. These men wanted a woman that would love and care for his children. He didn't want to get someone pregnant that operated in his world, not purposely anyway.

Mom has her own version of this tale and it goes a little something like this. "I was a church girl and I didn't know people like your dad. I remember once driving his Dually truck and he knew I had taken it to the beach without me ever telling him. He had eyes all over the place. I had no idea that I was dating a mob boss."

But mom would have to admit that during the 80's, a time when many blacks weren't doing well in this country, it was attractive to be with a young handsome black man with enough money to buy anything that he desired. And to be riding around Los Angeles in a Ferrari was radically different from anything most people in any hood had ever seen.

Despite their lifestyle differences, David and Robin's bond grew stronger with each passing day. They spent countless hours together, exploring the city and sharing their hope for the future.

One day, mom was at the grocery store once, and her ex-friend Karen tried to attack her. She fought off Karen and went straight to find David to get some answers. When she raised the issue, asking dad if he was still having a relationship with Karen. He insisted that he had broken it off with her, and he would demand that she stopped interfering in his life.

Young, handsome, rich men with no point of reference of fidelity, often allow their philandering to get in the way of their better judgment. For some, sleeping with numerous women dominate their existence. Dad wasn't any different. And he wasn't totally honest with my mother about breaking it off with Karen, evidenced by my younger sister Britany, Karen's daughter that's one year younger than I, which puts her birth between mine and Donovan's.

One fateful evening, Robin walked upon a scene that shattered her blissful ignorance. She accidentally stumbled upon a discussion between David and Michael, where their true identities were revealed as drug dealers. Shock and confusion swept over Robin, leaving her feeling betrayed and uncertain about her future with David. She confronted him, demanding answers. David, realizing the gravity of his secret coming to light, tried to reassure her that he would keep her safe and protect her from the dangers that surrounded his life.

I know mom had found her other half as evidenced in her remembering her days with him. "David was a man who thrived on luxury and had an insatiable appetite for life. His infectious enthusiasm radiated from his very pores. When I was around him, he was always a gentleman, even after I discovered the real way he was making money. He was the type of man that took care of his family. We never wanted for anything.

One of the many ways he expressed his zest for life was through his deep appreciation for music. Whenever he discovered an artist he loved, he would immerse himself in their music, playing it over and over again. I remember the soulful melodies and enchanting voice of Anita Baker being one of his favorites."

To learn about this information for the first time as I interviewed my mother was an eye-opener. Music, for me, is the universal language that connects souls and it speaks directly to my heart. This was evidence of how strong genetics can be as a huge smile burst across my face. I had grown up with friends never understanding the connection I could have with a record that would cause me to listen to it on repeat for hours. Now, I knew that my father understood, enhancing our father/son kinship. As many of the interviews had enlightened me more about just who my father was, this was another moment of awakening.

Mom had always told me that she had a vivid memory, and I would always think sure, until the retelling of this story. She remembered her time together with dad, down to the last details. "One memorable occasion was during our four-hour drive to Las Vegas. The open road stretched out before us as he sat behind the wheel, he pressed play on his car stereo, setting the stage for an unforgettable journey. It seemed like from the moment the soulful sounds of Anita Baker filled the car, Dave was transported to another realm. He sang along with every song, his voice harmonizing with Anita's, as if they were performing a duet. And I could tell that the lyrics spoke to him on a deeply personal level.

For a long period of time, it was like I wasn't even in the car, he seemed lost in a magical world where time and space ceased to exist, and only the music mattered, creating a soundtrack to the memories we would cherish forever.

Passersby along the highway was admiring his car but he didn't notice any of that, he was in his element and nothing or no one was going to disturb the peace he found there. It was a connection that ran deep within his soul.

When we drove into the valet at Caesar's Palace, the attendants were rushing to assist him. At that moment, I knew he spent a lot of time in that hotel because it was if they knew him personally. I saw David pass a bell hop a hundred-dollar bill and knew that probably had something to do with their almost extreme service.

When we walked through the doors of the hotel, hearing the crowd roar, he seemed to transform into a different person, a glint coming into his eyes that sparkled. I didn't understand what was going on but this place did have an aura of excitement.

We didn't even have to check-in. A host met us and escorted us to our suite. He asked was I hungry, which I was. We ordered room service, which was surprisingly good. Then we went down to the casino to the dice games. He found a spot at a crowded table of cheering people and wedged his way in. A chubby white man in a suit walked over to him, saying, "How are you doing tonight Mr. D?" I learned that the chubby man was a Pit boss, the supervisors of the crap games. It always amazed me that David seemed so bashful when people acknowledged him with respect. And he just nodded with his customary jolly smile.

And after a few minutes, I understood why that look had crossed his eyes. He was like a man possessed as he played Las Vegas craps. After a while, I got tired of just standing there, literally unnoticed, and told him I was going back to the suite. I don't know what time he came in but when I woke up, he was just getting out of the shower, drying his close-cropped hair. A few months prior to look more professional, he had decided to cut his trademark perm off.

David asked me did I want to go to breakfast. I showered and we went down to one of the hotel's restaurant. The waitresses were all over him, vying for his attention, and they didn't call him Mr. D, they called him David. And for the next two days, these activities were often repeated.

On our ride home, he slid in a Teddy Pendergrass cassette and this time I went to sleep, not wanting to sit through the same songs for four long hours. But I can say this, your dad's energy reminded me that life was meant to be lived with passion, curiosity, and an unwavering appreciation for the beauty that surrounds us."

As time went on, Robin began to notice aspects of David's personality that troubled her. His charm and magnetic presence attracted attention from other women, and Robin discovered that he had a history as a ladies' man. This revelation created a persistent sense of insecurity within her, and she found it increasingly difficult to trust David fully, especially after she became pregnant with his child.

The strains on their relationship grew, and Robin's doubt and fear began to overshadow the love they once shared. She questioned whether she could truly be with a man who led a life filled with deception, a man with a reputation for being unfaithful.

As the months passed, Robin's pregnancy progressed, and the weight of their circumstances pressed upon her. She struggled to reconcile her love for David with the reality of his past choices. The arrival of their son only intensified her desire for stability and a sense of security. David, aware of the growing wedge between them, made efforts to reassure Robin. He promised to change.

Young, handsome and rich men often allow their philandering to get in the way of their better judgment. Dad wasn't any different. One of his nicknames was King Midas, and like the saying associated with King Midas, I'm sure my dad felt that everything he touched turned to gold. If we all have a purpose on earth, in his short time here, he seemed to fulfill the purpose of bringing joy to everyone he touched, except maybe mom and other women that desired him to be only theirs.

Of course, I understand my mom's position, if for no other reason than loving her dearly. Dad was a player, leaving a trail of heartbroken women in his wake. He left me his good looks and in my younger years, I also caused a few hearts to ache.

Growing up, King Midas was the first alias name that I ever heard associated with dad, which planted the seed in my head that I was the Golden Child. I had been birthed with the touch of Midas, and this became my inspiration to put my best foot forward every day.

Mom, being a good church girl, couldn't understand why this was happening to her, and she completely ran away from the situation. "With knowledge of his cheating, I needed to get away. I definitely didn't want to bring you into the world in the midst of all of that so I left for San Francisco to stay with Auntie Dottie. I needed some space.

Of course, he was there by that weekend, sweet talking me to come home. He lost his wallet and someone returned. He marveled over that, saying we needed to move into a neighborhood like that. I laughed at how that small gesture of genuineness impressed him. But then I realized that would never happen in the world that he lived in.

My love for David remained steadfast, and I decided to give our relationship another chance. Over time, we built a life together, and he always provided for me and our growing family. It wasn't long before I was pregnant with your brother. He purchased a beautiful condo in the upscale neighborhood of Los Angeles known as the Don's, a token of his commitment to me, you and his unborn child.

Over time, David gradually tried to distance himself from his illicit activities, at least he said he was. But I witnessed him immersing himself in entrepreneurship, channeling his street smarts and resourcefulness into building successful businesses."

Over the years as I heard my dad's friends talk about his entrepreneurial exploits, thoughts were planted. And as they grew in my mind, they became a blueprint and probably the reason I was almost seamlessly able to start businesses.

Even in the course of time and despite dad's efforts, mom struggled to let go of her fears and doubts. The wounds of his past infidelities and the constant reminders of his previous life lingered, causing her to question whether she could ever fully trust him.

David's love for Robin and their son remained unwavering, and he understood the pain he had caused her. He was determined to make amends and prove himself worthy of her trust.

His businesses flourished, providing financial stability and security for their family. He used his success to create a nurturing and loving environment for Robin and their son, going above and beyond to demonstrate his love and devotion every day.

Robin, witnessing David's transformation and the lengths he was willing to go to rebuild their relationship, slowly started to let go of her fears. She saw the genuine remorse in his eyes and the efforts he made to make amends for his past mistakes. It was a gradual process, but with time, forgiveness and healing began to replace her lingering doubts.

Their love grew stronger, and they learned to communicate openly and honestly, sharing their hopes, fears, and dreams. Their son (Me) became a symbol of their love and resilience, a constant reminder of the beautiful life they had built together.

In the Don's, David and Robin created a haven of love. Surrounded by the echoes of their past, they chose to redefine their future together, creating a nurturing and loving home far from the chaos of his world.

Mom remembered a very disturbing day. "Right as things were getting better, two men knocked at the door, telling me that my car had been hit. I just knew they were there to rob me because they probably thought David had money at my house. And I wasn't about to open the door. I was on the phone with Auntie Faye while they were trying to convince me to come outside. She called the police, then David. He rushed home.

Before he arrived, the police had come and left, assuring me that no one was lurking around. After David knew I was all right, he asked why did I let the police in with all the money wrappers on the table. The precious night he had counted hundreds of thousands of dollars and left the wrappers for me to clean up. But the first thing I thought was, why does that matter? Then I realized that the police seeing that many money wrappers would suspect something. I was so scared that I hadn't even thought about the wrappers.

A few days later, David called and told me that he wouldn't be around for a minute and told me that I shouldn't go to work. He left some money and he would let me know when everything was okay. I think he was figuring out a way to handle the problem of whoever showed up uninvited at our house.

I was so out of the loop about his business affairs, that he went to the county jail for ninety days during my pregnancy and I never really knew why. But he could have just been with another woman and used jail as an excuse. His life was so foreign to me.

A few days after he came back, we went out to dinner with LaRue and Yvette. We would go out to dinner with them all the time. LaRue had become like a brother to me. Whenever I couldn't find your dad, I would call him and minutes later I would be on the phone with David. Their relationship was so strong that I think it caused Yvette and I to become friends. And Yvette and I were pregnant at the same time. When you were born, it just seemed natural for them to be your godparents. We had an official christening at our church to make it official.

From time to time, we would also go out with Terry and Lily. I would sometimes go get a car from Terry's lot to drive around in something different. But Terry talked too fast for me. And I always felt that a person that talked fast was trying to be deceptive in some way.

One of the things I hated most was when your dad would take you with him. I knew he drove too fast and didn't pay the greatest attention when he was driving. On a couple occasions he almost ran over someone on the street. Plus, he would fall asleep while driving. He would even fall asleep in the bath tub.

Once he almost hit someone on Slauson Avenue and I said, "Jumping Jehoshaphat," and that made him chuckle hard. He laughed at my mannerisms a lot.

We were leaving the mall one day, and I was eating on the type of candy that I liked. He asked for some, sticking his hand in the bag, and rushed the candy into his mouth, yuck, he said, then threw the rest back into the bag.

Your dad said, I think you buy nasty stuff so no one will ask you for any. I almost choked on the Sesame stick I was eating. He said, let me taste some of that, its got to be better than that candy. He tasted it and hated it.

During Memorial Day, that awful day, he tried to take you with him on the boat. A thought flashed through my mind of you repeatedly saying, daddy go fast, boom boom boom! So, I said no, and was adamant about that decision. He told you that he would see you later and that he loved you before he left.

Stacey and I were going to a birthday party later that same day. And on the way to the party, we were driving past Inglewood cemetery and I got this eerie feeling. I thought it was because it was Memorial Day weekend around the same time that LaRue was killed and he was buried in Inglewood cemetery.

When we got home from the party, Maa-maa said people have been continuously calling for me. Katherine called a couple of times. Yvette called a couple of times too.

I finally got in contact with Katherine, your dad's cousin, and she began asking a lot of questions about where had I been. After I told her, she said in a puzzling sounding voice, they can't find Dave.

Almost afraid to ask, I said, what do you mean they can't find him?

He drowned and they can't find the body.

I was so shocked that I dropped the phone, and began running through the house. My mom followed me, asking me what was wrong. I just kept moving erratically. Then she finally yelled at me to stop. Katherine was still on the phone but I had completely shut down and couldn't talk anymore.

Deucy came to the house with another one of their cousins and I questioned him. Deucy explained that the currents kept sucking him under and every time he would surface, something would pull him back under, until he got too tired to fight any longer, and began to float away.

When Yvette called and asked had I heard. I had. Everyone was either at Fannie's house in Leimert Park, the house that Dave and Mike had bought for her, or were on their way there. But I wasn't the type of woman that needed a lot of people around me to find comfort. I went within and communed with God to find comfort.

A few days later, I called your Aunt Star to find out if she wanted to go to the movies or something to get our minds off the tragedy, and as we were talking, the phone dropped. I called her back and asked was someone there. When she said yes, I told her I would call her back. I called Deucy and he went to check on her. I learned later that men were in the house, asking her where was the money.

Of course, with your dad gone, a deep hole was left in my heart but I had two boys that looked just him and this provided a source of comfort. I would always have a part of David Harris.

FREEWAY RICK

When I finally got the chance to meet Freeway Rick, he was everything I didn't expect. He had been a cult figure in LA for as long as I could remember. His face could be often found on his social media sites and on interviews with Vlad, Revolt TV's, Drink Champs, and many other media platforms. He had a genuine personality, not the Big-Willie fake attitude of most reputed drug kingpins.

As soon as we met, he made me feel like a hustler all over again. His energy was on another level and he seemed to have a million ideas on how to get rich. By this time, my youthful ambition of being a drug dealer was far behind me. I was the Director of Operations at Oxy Respiratory and Home Medical Equipment, making a great salary with a three percent profit split once the company hit its quota.

Freeway had such great admiration for my dad that he immediately asked me if I wanted a job. And I never turn down an opportunity for some extra cash. Babies need milk. When I said yes, he gave me a bundle of T-shirts.

I sold shirts with "The Real Rick Ross is not a Rapper" across the front, his admonition to impostors using his name. The salesman technique that I guess I inherited would sell out of the shirts in a few hours.

Working for Rick, gave me the opportunity to do direct sales again.

And this reminded me of my past fast money days, except this time it was completely legit.

My strategy included leveraging established brands and creating a rapport with consumers, to drive sales. The time I spent working for Rick was a major factor in elevating my thinking. It inspired me. And I understood later that the experience helped me on my next move of getting into the big game of the music industry.

As Freeway recounted his time with my father, I was impressed by his candidness. "I met Dave around 1983. In those days, they called men like us go-getters, men willing to risk it all to escape poverty. We were both considered go-getters. I loved that in myself so I loved that in him as well. Rappers like Ice Cube, NWA, Mack 10 and Snoop rapped about street hustlers lives.

We were amongst an ever-growing population of young black men that were willing to risk everything to defeat poverty. Even before I met Dave, I heard about a young player from the Bottoms that was getting it. And when we met, he told me a similar story about hearing my name ringing around town.

Although many tried to copy us but only a few had real salesman talent." Those of us who did have real talent, used to use the phrase, "I can sell snow to an Eskimo."

"But good dope sold itself because we had what a User desired. It was simply math – supply and demand. It wasn't long before people like he and I had an abundant supply. And those of us that were serious about becoming wealthy didn't get high on our own supply.

But amongst those that sold this product, rarely did that same person also sell to the dealers. Dave was the favorite drug dealers, drug dealer. Simply put, he was just a well-loved guy.

Big Palace of Wheels was one of my many legitimate business ventures. And one day Dave came by to buy some accessories for his car. If a black man could afford a Mercedes or Cadillac in those times, he had to dress it up, which meant he put an additional ten to fifty thousand in accessories on it – anything from shiny rims to specialized tires. And I had whatever players needed at my shop.

Dave was driving a Ferrari and I think he needed some new Pirelli tires, some of the most expensive tires in the world. He also bought the friend that was with him a set of Zenith and Vogue tires for his Cadillac.

We chatted as I walked them to their cars and Dave saw my boat. As he was admiring it, I invited him out on a boat ride that afternoon. I brought along a few of my lady friends to give the outing a little more excitement.

I was backing the boat, still attached to my truck, into the water, when Dave arrived. I loved being out on the water and I wanted to share this special treat with my new friend so he could experience the thrill of a speed boat ride. I haven't ever experienced anything as exhilarating in my entire life.

Dave walked over, and I introduced him. And of course, his charm took center stage as he shook both lady's hand, saying, "Pleasure to meet you both."

Then he helped me get the boat in the water. We all hopped in and I cruised the boat through the harbor. As soon as I made it to deep waters, I gunned it, causing the boat to sit on top of the water. The women screamed and when I looked over at Dave, his eyes were lit up. There was no denying that he was a speed demon like me. And I was glad he was having a good time."

I already knew that dad was a thrill seeker but, on this day, I would learn that Rick, equally had a need for speed. With both men being thrill seekers, they were always seeking out new adventures and experiences, and on this particular sunny afternoon, they found themselves on Freeway's sleek and powerful vessel, perfectly designed for high-speed rides across the water.

As dad looked out at the sparkling blue expanse before them, he couldn't help but feel a surge of excitement. The lovely ladies that Freeway invited were equally thrilled to be a part of this experience, and their pretty giggles filled the air.

Freeway couldn't resist the temptation to push the boat to its limits. With a mischievous smile, he gripped the steering wheel tightly, his fingers itching to feel the rush of the wind against his face. Dave, always up for a good thrill, eagerly encouraged him.

The boat's engine roared loudly as Freeway gunned the throttle more. The powerful motor propelled them forward, and the boat sliced through the water, leaving a trail of white foam in its wake. The wind whipped around them, tugging at their hair and clothes, adding to the exhilaration of the moment.

Dad and Freeway exchanged glances and shared a knowing smile. They were in their element, living life on the outer edge, and relishing every second of it. The boat zoomed across the marina, weaving between other boats with expert precision. The onlookers couldn't help but be captivated by this display of skill and sheer enjoyment.

The laughter and excitement on Freeway's boat grew with each passing moment. The women clung to each other, their eyes sparkling with a mixture of fear and exhilaration. They felt alive, their hearts pounding in sync with the rhythmic roar of the engine.

Freeway skillfully maneuvered the boat, navigating the twists and turns of the marina with ease as he reveled in the feeling of power and control, his instincts honed by years of experience on the water. The boat seemed to respond to his every command, gliding effortlessly across the surface.

As they sped along, one of the ladies went below and returned with some snacks. Time flew by as they continued their high-speed adventure, while enjoying their snacks. The sun began to cast long shadows over the marina, signaling the approaching evening. Reluctantly, Freeway eased off the throttle, gradually slowing the boat down.

As the boat glided back to the marina, they were greeted by a round of applause and cheers from the onlookers who had witnessed this exhilarating display. The women on the boat exchanged knowing glances, their faces flushed with excitement and their hair tousled by the wind.

Dad and Freeway shared a triumphant high-five, their eyes shining with a sense of accomplishment. They had embraced the freedom of the open water, the thrill of the speed, and the joy of sharing the experience with each other.

Rick's stories left me wanting to go on a high-speed boat ride as he continued, his storytelling vivid. "When we made it to shore, I asked Dave what did he think and he said, can I buy it? I just laughed, knowing how my first speed boat ride had left me the same way. After flying through the water, I had to have a boat. I agreed only because I had recently purchased a brand-new cigarette boat.

Me, Dave and a few other of our friends that owned boats decided to take our boats out for the Memorial Day weekend 1988. We were cruising Catalina with hundreds of other boats, everyone having a wonderful time when our joyful day suddenly took a turn for the worse as an unexpected storm rolled in, prompting a wind advisory from the Coast guard. As we hurriedly made our way towards the shore, I noticed that Dave's boat was adrift, seemingly in distress. Reacting quickly, I signaled the other boaters and we circled back to assist our friend.

As we approached Dave's boat, it became apparent that he was in serious trouble. We began shouting for Dave and his companion, Deucy, to abandon the boat. Two brave men from Dave's boat leaped into the water and were successfully rescued by one of the nearby boats. But neither Dave nor Deucy were visible. A few minutes later, someone managed to snatch Deucy before the boat sank, and both of them were eventually rescued from the water.

As we watched the sinking boat, "I felt helpless that I couldn't save Dave." The way Rick's story ended left me heartbroken all over again. But even with these interviews, leaving my emotions feeling tossed to and fro, I felt a burning desire to complete the mission.

INTRUSION

While the country was experiencing the devastating effect of this highly addictive and potent form of cocaine rapidly infiltrating many urban neighborhoods, leading to waves of violence, addiction, and social upheaval that left an ugly stain on the city. Its easy accessibility led to a surge in drug use while powerful street gangs warred to control areas that had a thriving drug trade. Neighborhoods once known for their vibrant communities became battlegrounds.

Some people that once watered their lawns and kept them manicured, now chased after a cocaine high as evidenced by their unkempt yards and the collapse of productive communities all over LA.

During this time, the Kartier Boys' reputation preceded them, and few dared to encroach upon their territory. However, as with any empire, there were always those who sought to claim the throne for themselves.

The Kartier Boys had established 46th and Central as their headquarters, turning it into a thriving area for crack sales. Another clique wanted a piece of the action with their sights on expanding their own empire.

Men that they had thought to be allies, had attempted to encroach upon their territory by establishing a new rock spot on 46th and Central, the Kartier Boys' home turf, but their audacious move had provoked a swift and dangerous response.

The members inside of the neighbor's house that they intended to establish a stronghold, found themselves face to face with the business end of Big Tommy's shotgun, sending a clear message.

Dave spent a lot of time with one of their leaders. He had even tried to date one of their beautiful sisters and felt betrayed by this takeover scheme. And the Kartier Boys were not willing to relinquish their territory without a fight. This move caused a response and the two sides were destined to clash with the potential of it escalating into an all-out war.

Their clique had about 40 gang members within their ranks. Understanding the need for reinforcement, Dave made a call to his trusted friend Stevie Robinson, who ran Whitey's Enterprise, a clique inside of the 5-Deuce Broadway's street gang. Dave, a wise and pragmatic leader, understood the importance of maintaining peace within the community but the opposers had gone too far. Everyone recognized the potential of the devastation a gang war would bring.

Their once-unquestioned authority was now in question, and the incident had attracted unwanted attention from law enforcement agencies. News of the beef between the Kartier Boys and their group spread like wildfire throughout the city. The police, eager to make a high-profile arrest, intensified their efforts to crack down on both groups, bringing increased scrutiny to the Kartier Boys.

Dave understood the gravity of the situation. He knew that the repercussions of their actions would be far-reaching and potentially catastrophic for their operations. It was time to regroup, strategize, and come away with a winning solution.

With a commitment to preventing unnecessary bloodshed, their leader agreed to meet with Black Dave. At a restaurant in a neutral location, away from the prying eyes of their respective groups, he and Dave engaged in a peaceful negotiation. Both men had known each other for a while and they both knew there was room for dialogue, understanding, and the pursuit of common ground. Both men understood the weight of their decisions and the impact they had on their respective groups.

They recognized if their disagreement escalated to a full-scale war, it would only lead to further violence and the slowing down of profits. After they had finished their meal, the two of them decided to call a truce, putting an end to the brewing conflict. The news was met with relief and cautious optimism within their respective groups, as the prospect of peace offered a different result in an otherwise volatile landscape. Word spread that the beef had been squashed.

The ability to put aside differences and prioritize peace set an example for others around the city to follow. As the days turned into weeks, the tension that once hung in the air slowly dissipated, replaced by a newfound sense of cooperation. This signified that peace was not an unattainable dream but a tangible reality worth striving for.

In many instances, Uncle Mike and Uncle Tommy were polar opposites of my dad's diplomacy, which set up a nice mix of good guy/bad guy, leaving everyone guessing. Uncle Mike knew they would have to face this type of dispute again, and it wouldn't be solved this easily.

This struggle transformed the young men. They emerged scarred but wiser, ready to face the challenges that lay ahead. Over time, they managed to weather the storm as the men managed to maintain their power and influence over the block. And the police attention gradually shifted elsewhere.

However, the rival takeover attempt had left a lasting impact on the Kartier Boys. They became more cautious, constantly on guard for any signs of renewed aggression or internal betrayal. The boys knew that the city was watching, other groups just waiting for the opportune moment to strike against any semblance of weakness.

The repercussions of the conflict taught them valuable lessons about the precarious nature of their empire. They understood that power could be fleeting and that complacency could lead to their downfall. The rival takeover attempt had served as a wake-up call, a stark reminder that they needed to evolve and adapt to survive in the ever-changing landscape of organized crime.

Trust was at a premium, having to be earned and proven, and any signs of disloyalty or association with rival factions were dealt with swiftly and ruthlessly. Everyone was aware that a homeboy would kill his own homeboy for the right price.

But the Kartier Boys were known as a tightly-knit brotherhood, with each member aware of the consequences of betraying their own. Mike implemented a "no smokers allowed" policy, which meant if you used crack or even sniffed powder you couldn't be amongst the ranks. And if someone chose to violate this policy, he would be dealt with severely.

As the days turned into months, the Kartier Boys gradually regained their footing. Their presence remained a formidable force, and whispers of the failed rival takeover attempt served as a reminder to those who dared to challenge their reign.

They understood that the world of organized crime was a constant battle for dominance. Rivals would always emerge, seeking to stake their claim and challenge the established order. The repercussions of the rival takeover attempt had taught them that staying on top required vigilance, adaptability, and an undying commitment to protecting their interests.

MOVE TO WATTS

Uncle Michael and his unrelenting ambition, had expansion plans. Although the brothers disagreed on many issues, their personalities totally different. But Dave's thirst for more wealth never disagreed with Mike's schemes to get richer.

Law enforcement on their side of town knew them by name, and had begun repeatedly harassing them. And for their mother's safety, they knew that they needed to get their underworld business dealings away from her.

Officer Goldberg, a prominent figure at the Newton police station, had developed an intense fixation on the Kartier Boys. Goldberg became consumed with a desire to bring them down and would stop at nothing to achieve his goal. His relentless pursuit led to a series of encounters that intensified the tension between law enforcement and the Kartier Boys.

Goldberg's newfound obsession with the young men manifested in a pattern of aggressive and unwarranted searches. He would pull his car to a screeching halt and jump out, rushing towards members of the Kartier Boys, demanding that they empty their pockets in the hopes of discovering evidence, particularly cocaine, that would provide grounds for arresting them. The boys grew increasingly frustrated and resentful, feeling harassed by Goldberg's tactics.

But they were aware of the limitations of their power, and understood that they couldn't walk on water and were vulnerable to the long arm of the law. They realized that they needed to take action to protect themselves and maintain their operations. Forced to relent to Goldberg's unyielding pursuit, Mike made a crucial decision: to relocate and move outside of the officer's jurisdiction. The process of relocation was not an easy one. It involved meticulous planning, strategic alliances, and a careful evaluation of potential new territories.

But driven by their need to elude police, Mike set his sights on the Westside of Los Angeles, a land of opportunity and untapped potential. He sought for safe harbors in neighborhoods where they could establish a fresh base of operations, away from Goldberg's watchful eyes.

As the mastermind behind their operations, Mike decided to make a strategic move into Watts. This move was accompanied by a sense of uncertainty and apprehension. He knew that leaving their established territory meant leaving behind familiar surroundings, connections, and the sense of control they once had. But he was willing to take the risk in order to escape a possible prison sentence.

Uncle Mike called a meeting to let everyone know about their move. "The police is breathing down our next down here. They know us by name. So, it's time for us to make a move to Watts. Anyone that has 100k can partner with Dave and I on this undertaking. Dave will handle the supplies, and whoever our new partner is today will help me with the spots."

None of the fellows were ready, not even Deucy who had been with them since the beginning. Big Tommy was the only one of a dozen members that was ready to invest in this new business venture.

Mike and Dave had always been known as kings on the Eastside, operating their illicit operations around the unforgiving streets of 46th and Central in Los Angeles. Their reputation for ruthless efficiency, coupled with their unwavering loyalty to family, had earned them a place of respect in the city's criminal underworld. But now, it was time to venture into an uncharted territory – Watts.

The next day Mike and Dave met with Stanley Levi, a young man from Watts at Fannie Mae's Café to discuss the move into his territory. There was a major gang that controlled most of the underworld activities in that area and Levi assured them safe passage.

Levi told me during his interview. "I was glad that they invited me to meet them at Fannie Mae's Café. Their mama made the best sausage and eggs in the city. You could tell that a lot of love went into her cooking. Looking at Mike and Dave's mama at work, cooking meals, I knew that's where their hustle game came from. You could just sense that she was a lady that about her business.

Dave didn't say much that day but Mike knew what he wanted to do. I had a spot on 104th and San Pedro that we would convert into a rock spot.

The next day, Mike, Dave and Tommy pulled. And we went to work. I knew two brothers, Lil T and Tito that were from the neighborhood gang and Mike recruited Damon and Lil Mike. And these four men would take shifts at the spot.

From the day we opened the doors, the money started rolling in. We directed the customers to the backyard and we served them out of a bedroom window. We would divvy up the money, hundreds of thousands of dollars, every Sunday. Mike, Dave, Tommy, and myself would count the profits on a king-sized bed at one of your father's locations on 74th and Figueroa. This seemingly ordinary house would serve as their newest stash spot, a hidden hub for our expanding empire.

Dave was always reserved, watching everything very careful. His demeanor told me that he was a serious individual. But most of my dealings were either with Mike or Tommy.

One notorious story about the house on 104th was the time that we ran out of work (cocaine). And the backyard was filled with people waiting for their elixir. Tommy got the bright idea to start a barbecue. Tito was given money to go to the market to purchase a variety of meats, bread, charcoal and paper plates. As soon as he returned, the grill was fired up. The volume of the music was turned up and we had a party.

The crack arrives and Tito and Damon began selling them rocks from the back window. Customers left with a plate of barbeque, along with their rock cocaine."

As the Kartier Boys settled into their new environment, they saw it as an opportunity for reinvention. They focused on rebuilding their networks, establishing new alliances, and adapting their operations to the new challenges they faced. The experience of being uprooted from their previous territory served as a wake-up call, prompting them to reassess their strategies and strengthen their resilience.

The Westside presented a different landscape for the Kartier Boys. Here, the drug addicts included not only the usual suspects but also entertainers seeking an escape from their glamorous yet demanding lives. Rumors circulated that even a professional boxer, seeking a dangerous thrill beyond the ring, had fallen into the clutches of addiction. It was a world where the lines between the glamorous and the desperate blurred, and the Kartier Boys saw an opportunity to exploit these vulnerabilities.

But soon the gang that ran the area, posed a potential threat to the Kartier Boys' expansion plans. Dad had established a good rapport with some of the top members of their gang. It was a vulnerable balance of cooperation and competition, as they employed men from the gang to work for them. This strategic alliance allowed them to handle the fickle environment of the gang's hood, while ensuring their own survival.

As their operations flourished, the Kartier Boys' wealth and status skyrocketed. Their empire expanded like wildfire, reaching far beyond the Westside. They opened new spots all across Los Angeles, from the notorious neighborhoods of Compton to streets in Long Beach to even a few spots in the Jungles, an area dominated by a Blood gang.

For over five years, the Kartier Boys reigned supreme all over the City of Angels. Their empire thrived, fueled by their relentless pursuit of wealth and their unwavering loyalty to family. Their influence extended far and wide, ascending over the entire criminal landscape of Los Angeles.

But as with any empire built on the foundation of illegality, cracks begin to form beneath the surface. Rivalries simmered, alliances grew strained, and the line between friend and foe blurred. The Kartier Boys knew that maintaining their dominance would require even more cunning, ruthlessness, and sacrifice.

Little did they know that their reign, though seemingly unassailable, would soon face its greatest challenges yet. The Westside, once their land of opportunity, would become a battleground where loyalties would be tested, alliances shattered, and blood spilled. The men would soon discover that the price of power came at a cost higher than they could have ever imagined.

Their expansion into the Westside had proven to be a lucrative move, as their influence spread like wildfire across LA, Compton, and Long Beach. Yet, within the shadows of their success, seeds of betrayal were sown, threatening to unravel everything they had built.

The gang that dominated the area, once considered allies, began to show signs of restlessness. Their top members, who had once shared a camaraderie with Dad and Uncle Mike, now eyed the Kartier Boys' power and wealth with envy. The allure of control and dominance proved too tempting for some, igniting a murderous spark within the ranks of their gang.

Unbeknownst to the Kartier Boys, whispers of dissent echoed through the streets they once controlled. A deadly plot was brewing, fueled by greed and ambition. As their empire expanded, so did the number of enemies seeking to topple them from their throne.

Once a promised land of opportunity, Watts now proved to be a double-edged sword. Gang members from the area felt the turf belonged to them, and the police was determined to run both groups out of the area.

CRASH

During these times, the city of Los Angeles found itself in the grip of a rampant drug epidemic and escalating gang violence. The streets were plagued by the activities of numerous street gangs, and drug dealers seemed to be multiplying at an alarming rate. And with their tremendous wealth, they built armies and fortified them with the latest high-tech weaponry.

The situation demanded a strong response from law enforcement, and it was in this climate that the notorious law enforcement unit known as CRASH (Community Resources Against Street Hoodlums) emerged. CRASH was a specialized task force within the Los Angeles Police Department (LAPD) and was created to combat a twin threat: the rising tide of illicit drug sales and gangs in Watts.

Police started kicking in doors of spots and also pulling men over and searching their cars and pockets. There station for the 44th District was at the top of a Boys Market on Manchester Avenue.

This unit was established under the leadership of Police Chief Daryl Gates, a controversial figure known for his tough-on-crime stance. To rally public support and secure additional resources, CRASH adopted a strategic approach. They falsely labeled all drug dealers in Los Angeles as gang members, blurring the lines between the two issues and presenting them as interconnected problems. By doing so, this task squad aimed to garner the support of the community and policymakers, who would be more inclined to allocate additional resources to fight a war on two fronts.

The unit consisted of a highly trained and motivated group of officers who were handpicked based on their experience, street smarts, and dedication to the cause. Equipped with specialized training and resources, these officers were known for their aggressive tactics and relentless pursuit of drug dealers and gang members. They were given a wide range of powers to operate with a certain degree of autonomy, enabling them to swiftly respond to emerging threats and dismantle criminal networks.

These officers integrated themselves deeply into the communities they served, working closely with residents and community leaders to gather intelligence, build trust, and establish strong networks of informants. They patrolled gang-infested neighborhoods, conducting frequent raids, making arrests, and seizing drugs and weapons. In their relentless pursuit, these officers often walked a fine line between upholding the law and bending it to achieve their ends.

According to Big Tommy, Mike was light years ahead of men his age in his thinking. Uncle Mike had the foresight to see that they couldn't continue selling drugs right out in the open, and he begin opening legal businesses to wash all the illegitimate money that was pouring in. "Michael took the initiative to launch Kartier Limousine service. He was two years older or more than everyone else in the crew and he felt it was his responsibility to keep all of us out of harm's way of the police as I felt it was my responsibility to keep us out of harm's way of the jackers or any perceived threat. Your dad always kept a level head even in the midst of controversy or war."

CRASH initially enjoyed considerable success in reducing drug-related crimes and disrupting gang activities, but their aggressive tactics and controversial methods soon attracted criticism and scrutiny. The line between targeting actual criminals and profiling innocent individuals became blurred, leading to allegations of racial profiling and civil rights abuses. Community trust, crucial for effective policing, deteriorated as many residents felt unfairly targeted by this task squad.

While the focus turned to disbanding the unit, the drug trade continued to thrive throughout the city, and other task squads were developed within other departments.

As the 1990s rolled in, the Rodney King incident and subsequent riots intensified the public scrutiny on law enforcement practices in Los Angeles. The LAPD faced mounting pressure to address the allegations of misconduct and excessive use of force. In the wake of these events, the unit became a focal point of criticism and calls for reform.

In 2000, a scandal erupted within the unit when it was revealed that some CRASH officers had engaged in corruption, theft, and even murder. This revelation further tarnished the reputation of the unit and led to its eventual disbandment. The fallout from the scandal resulted in widespread reforms within the LAPD and a renewed focus on community policing and building trust with the communities it served.

Around this same time, another group of rogue police were being arrested. The Rampart scandal, another dark chapter in the history of the Los Angeles Police Department during the late 1990s, had been uncovered. The scandal revolved around the Rampart Division, exposing a network of corruption and misconduct involving several officers. Notable figures among them included Rafael Pérez, an LAPD officer who became a key informant, and David Mack, a former officer who had ties to the infamous bank robbery at the Bank of America in North Hollywood. The scandal revealed a disturbing pattern of drug dealing, evidence planting, racial profiling, and unjustified uses of force, severely damaging the reputation of the LAPD and eroding public trust.

The legacy of CRASH and other units like it remain controversial, the harm done by rogue officers irreparable to a community that trusted police to be honest and fair. Although its creation exemplified the desperate measures taken by law enforcement to reclaim the streets, there was not a need for the corruption. The tactics employed by this unit and the subsequent fallout serve as a lasting reminder of the needed balance between public safety and individual rights that law enforcement must navigate.

In the aftermath of this and other scandals, the Los Angeles Police Department underwent a comprehensive overhaul. Reforms were implemented to address the issues of corruption, misconduct, and racial profiling within the ranks. The focus shifted towards building stronger relationships with the communities they served, fostering trust, and promoting transparency.

Community policing became a central tenet of the LAPD's new approach. Officers were encouraged to engage with residents, attend community meetings, and collaborate with community organizations to address the root causes of crime. The goal was to establish partnerships that would empower communities to take an active role in crime prevention and ensure that policing efforts were more inclusive and equitable.

Out of these ashes emerged a renewed commitment to addressing the complex issues of drugs and gangs in Los Angeles. The LAPD recognized that the problems could not be solved through heavy-handed tactics alone. A multi-faceted approach was adopted, combining law enforcement efforts with social programs, education, and community development initiatives.

The dismantling of CRASH and other similar units also led to the creation of specialized units that focused on targeted enforcement against gangs and drug-related crimes. However, these new units operated within a framework that emphasized collaboration and respect for individual rights. Intelligence-driven policing strategies were implemented, with a greater emphasis on gathering accurate information and conducting thorough investigations before taking action.

The reforms within the LAPD were not without challenges. Rebuilding trust with the communities that had been most affected by aggressive policing practices took time and required a sustained commitment to change. The scars left by CRASH were deep, and many individuals remained skeptical of law enforcement's intentions.

Over the years, the LAPD made significant strides in improving its relationship with the community. Officers received training in cultural sensitivity, de-escalation techniques, and implicit bias to ensure fair and equitable treatment of all residents. Accountability mechanisms were strengthened, and community oversight boards were established to provide civilian input and hold the police accountable for their actions.

As the new millennium progressed, the LAPD's efforts began to yield positive results. Crime rates, particularly those related to drugs and gangs, started to decline. The collaborative approach between law enforcement and the community proved to be more effective in preventing crime and addressing the underlying issues that contributed to it.

Today, the legacy of CRASH and other rogue units serve as a cautionary tale – a reminder that even in the face of pressing challenges, law enforcement must always uphold the principles of justice, fairness, and respect for individual rights.

TERRY CARTER

My mom never like how fast Terry talked but I admired it. He was a slick-talking salesman and great at it. Terry Carter, whom I call TC, was the owner of Word Class Auto a car dealership in Inglewood. Terry told me that my dad and LaRue Sr. had desk at his company though there were rarely used.

Terry and my dad hit it off and quickly became good friends. Terry was one of dad's means to accomplish their dream of being legitimate. After my dad's death, he was heavily involved in my life. He told me about many adventures that he and my dad went on. His business savvy was impressive.

Terry was well respected by members of blood gangs. He was raised in Compton, California, in an area dominated by Pirus.

My Godfather Terry's life ended bizarrely. He was tragically ran over by a car, the driver being known other than Suge Knight, the same fellow that had tried to swindle my uncle out of his record company, the same fellow that was in the car the night Tupac was killed, the same fellow that ruined the greatest hip hop company the world has ever seen.

It is so ironic that Suge Knight, the man that my uncle Mike was embroiled in a battle with over the rights of his company, Death Row Records, would be the same man that was found guilty for murdering my Godfather Terry and on a completely unrelated matter from my uncle's.

Uncle Terry and Aunt Lillian, an integral part of our extended family, always encouraged me to do my very best. Terry gave me an internship as a creative/designer at Keep It Pushin' Entertainment. My tasks ranged from calling program directors at radio stations to get our records played, to artist artwork for advertisement/promotions. I worked closely with artists like Dirty Blac, Jay Rock, Rythme D. Working at Keep It Pushin' Entertainment was my intro into the inner workings of the music industry.

I would often visit with Terry and his family at their house in Ladera Heights. From my earliest memory, his house was always a place that many of kids my age and younger called felt home. I felt so proud every time I saw a black married couple, thriving, and taking care of their family. To me, it looked like something from a television series. Uncle Terry's household, the Carter's house, was a wholesome blend of Fresh Prince of Bellaire, Black-ish and Run's House.

When I was younger, being at Terry's house were some of my fondest times. He always had something exciting to do: Slip N' Slide, Bounce House, or Video games. I would accompany him sometimes to his lowrider shop. It was amazing for me, as it is for most Los Angeles black kids, to see what we call "hitting the switches." When the switch was hit, it caused the lowrider to leap from the ground. I know, it's a LA thang!

I followed TC everywhere, even to some of his business meetings. Watching the intricate behind-the-scenes details, was exciting while very instructive. The most important part of all of this for me, was seeing a solid patriarch at work, and how that affected all aspects of his family's life. I could see a reflection of his personality in his children.

His presence brought a unique blend of wisdom, charisma, and a touch of stability to my young years. Whenever Terry entered a room, it seemed as if the atmosphere transformed, filled with his lively conversations and laughter. Memories of Uncle Terry helped me to create my businessman temperament as I began to set my blueprint in motion.

Uncle Terry, in particular, played a significant role in shaping my understanding of my family's name and the world of business. He was the kind of uncle who took me under his wing, sharing his experiences and imparting valuable life lessons. He understood the importance of my family's legacy and the responsibility that came with it.

He was the first person that told me that I was a member of a proud family. A family that was respected all over the city. In a city that was divided by gang turfs, Terry said my dad could go into any neighborhood and be perfectly safe.

I remember vividly the day told me about some of my father and uncle Mike's exploits. We stood by his car, a sleek black Mercedes that seemed to exude success and sophistication. As we walked around it, he shared stories about how my father was such a carefree soul, the exact opposite of my uncle, who was a very serious individual. He asked, "You do know that your biological uncle, Mike, founded Death Row Records, the largest Hip-Hop record label in the 90s?" I shook my head to confirm that I did.

"Just as your Uncle Mike," Uncle Terry began, his voice mixed with tinge of admiration, "made waves in the music industry, building an empire, leaving a lasting impact on the Hip-Hop world. You carry that legacy within you."

His words sparked a sense of curiosity within me. Uncle Terry recognized my eagerness to learn, nurturing it with patience and guidance. He became my first mentor in the business world, teaching me valuable lessons as we strolled through the streets or sat in his office, surrounded by books and paperwork.

When I walked into Terry's office, I often marveled over how it stood out over many other offices I had entered. As I took the stairs to his main office that was located above his lowrider shop, I passed plaques of collaborative work he had done with the rapper/movie star/entrepreneur Ice Cube.

His staff was some of the most pleasant people I had ever met, which I felt was a reflection of their boss. Terry's record label Heavyweight Records, frequently collaborated with Ice Cube, producing songs like: "We Be Clubbin'" and "Pushin' Weight." These songs featured Terry's artist, Mr. Short Khop.

Terry was an executive producer on "The Player's Club" soundtrack which featured Ice Cube, DMX, Scarface & Jay-Z. Heavyweight Records also released Mr. Short Khop's album "Da Khop Shop" which included hits like "Dollaz, Dank & Drank" featuring Kokane, and received mainstream success. Da Khop Shop is still one of my favorite albums.

When Short Khop, recorded "MVP," Shaquille O'Neal (Shaq) featured. Blaqtoven was the producer, a producer now signed to my label – full circle. The video for the song was done at the Staple Center. This was the first time I witnessed a major production. With Shaq being involved, you know it was done professionally with all the top-level producers and camera people. Shaq's entourage alone must have been over a hundred people.

Uncle Terry always emphasized to me the importance of legitimacy in the business world. He believed that success should be achieved through hard work, integrity, and ethical practices. He often spoke about the pitfalls of taking shortcuts or relying on dubious methods to get ahead. I felt these speeches were a direct result of my dad's lifestyle. Terry didn't want to see me travel down that road.

One day, over a cup of coffee, Uncle Terry shared a story about my dad's pursuit of legitimacy. He explained that when my dad first entered the business world, he was rough around the edges but in no time, he fit into the scene as if he was born into it. He said, Dave was smart, picking up anything that he was interested in with ease.

He admired my dad's tenacity and dedication. He saw how my dad's hard work paid off as he was transforming into a businessman. He emphasized that my dad's pursuit of legitimacy was not just about getting out of the drug game forever, but also about personal growth. In the pursuit of legitimacy, my father and Uncle Terry collaborated on numerous ventures, establishing legitimate businesses that thrived.

As I grew older, Uncle Terry's lessons and my dad's example became ingrained in my own approach to life and business. I learned to value hard work, integrity, and the importance of earning success through my own efforts. I understood that our family's name was both a privilege and a responsibility, and it was up to me to uphold its legacy with honor.

His stories about his own ventures and successes painted a picture of determination and entrepreneurial spirit. He shared his experiences of running legitimate businesses. Through his and my dad's partnership, they had built a network of enterprises that reflected their vision of achieving success within the boundaries of the law.

I absorbed these lessons like a sponge, eager to understand the intricacies of the business world. Uncle Terry's tales of strategic decision-making, financial management, and the importance of building a strong reputation left an indelible mark on my young mind. He instilled in me the belief that one could strive for greatness while maintaining integrity and honor.

But it wasn't just business that Uncle Terry spoke about. He also regaled me with stories of the good times he and my father had shared. They were inseparable, a dynamic duo that embraced life's adventures with open arms. From spontaneous trips to Las Vegas to attend professional boxing matches to nights of laughter and camaraderie, their bond everlasting.

Uncle Terry's mischievous smile would widen as he shared anecdotes about my father's charisma and his way with the ladies. He recounted tales of their escapades, painting a picture of a life filled with excitement and unforgettable memories. Through these stories, I gained a deeper understanding of my father's spirit, his quest, and his ability to leave an impression on those around him.

As I reflect on those formative years, I realize that Uncle Terry was my father's bridge to a vision of complete legitimacy. He provided guidance and mentorship, nurturing my father's aspirations and helping him to maneuver in the complex world of business. It was through their partnership and friendship that my father moved closer to his dreams of building a life that was wholly legitimate and respected.

Terry's influence extended beyond the realm of business. He was a source of inspiration, reminding my father of the possibilities that lay before him and the importance of staying true to his ambitions. His unwavering support created a bond that went beyond blood ties.

He became not only a mentor for me but also a confidant as he had once been for my dad. We would sit together, sharing thoughts and dreams, discussing the challenges and triumphs of life. He encouraged me to pursue my own passions, imparting the wisdom he had gained from his own journey.

Through our conversations, I learned that success was not solely defined by financial achievements but by the impact we have on those around us. Uncle Terry emphasized the importance of leaving a positive legacy, of using my resources and abilities to uplift others and make a difference in the world.

As I look back on those years, I am filled with gratitude for the lessons Uncle Terry imparted and the impact he had on my father's life. His guidance not only shaped my father's journey but also influenced the way I perceive success, business, and personal growth.

Uncle Terry's passing left a void in our lives, but his legacy lives on in the lessons he taught and the memories we hold dear. His stories and the bond he shared with my father continue to inspire me to strive for greatness, to embrace opportunities with an open mind, and to leave a positive impact on those I encounter.

Today, as I walk the path of my own aspirations, I carry with me the spirit of Uncle Terry and my father. I honor their memory by upholding the values they instilled in me – integrity, resilience, and a commitment to making a difference. Their stories remind me that our family's name carries weight, and it is our duty to uphold its honor and continue the legacy of greatness.

Uncle Terry's life encompassed the essence of a life well-lived, one that embraced ambition, integrity, and the power of human connection. Terry's lessons and my dad's example became ingrained in my own approach to life and business. I learned to value hard work, integrity, and the importance of earning success through my own efforts. I understood that our family's name was both a privilege and a responsibility, and it was up to me to uphold its legacy with honor.

His lessons and my dad's pursuit of legitimacy shaped not just my understanding of business but also my character. I learned the value of authenticity, humility, and the power of determination. As I continue on my own path, I carry this wisdom within me, knowing that success is not just about achieving goals but also about staying true to oneself.

HIGHWAY ROBBERY

The same way other men trusted Dave with their money, he trusted others with his. As the story goes, Dave was re-upping for their organization with his Mexican plug, Jorge Garza.

They would meet at a hotel parking lot. Jorge told him that his Colombian connect didn't want to meet anyone new, persuading Dave to turn over the money to him so he could make the purchase. Dave had no problem giving him the buy money.

Jorge went into the hotel with a briefcase full of money. After an hour passed and he wasn't back, Dave recognized that he had been had. Apparently, Jorge had gone straight out the back door.

Dave called the spot to tell Mike about Jorge's thievery. As soon as Uncle Mike got the news to Uncle Tommy, he knew exactly what to do.

Uncle Tommy took Neff and Damon with him, and they drove directly to the restaurant where they knew Jorge's wife worked, information that they had gained from their secret surveillance of Jorge.

The men entered the restaurant, Uncle Tommy locking the deadbolt lock, then lowering the blinds. An audible gasp was released from several of the patrons when they saw the men's guns drawn. The patrons were told to remain calm and no one would be hurt. Uncle Tommy told them that he was just there for Jorge's woman.

Soon after those words was out of his mouth, she appeared from the back of the restaurant. "I'm Jorge's woman." She looked frightened. And for some reason it just seemed like she knew this was coming. Jorge had probably confided in her about his diabolical plan or either he had pulled this off before. Not this time!

Damon was instructed to bring the Van into the alley. Tommy and Neff rushed out with Jorge's woman through the kitchen. A short Mexican guy with a butcher knife in his hand looked as though he was about to try to defend her. "Put it down!" Uncle Tommy ordered.

The man acted as though he didn't understand English or maybe he didn't. But when his eyes met Uncle Tommy's nine-millimeter trained on his forehead, his resolve disappeared as he lowered his head. There was a possible language barrier but the *pistola* spoke volumes.

They loaded the woman in the back of the Van and Uncle Tommy took the seat opposite of her. Damon sped out of the alley, and straight to the freeway. On the ride to their secluded condo, Uncle Tommy explained to her why she was in her current predicament. Then he asked what was her name.

"Lupe." Lupe looked disappointed in her man. Maybe he hadn't told her. She was told once her husband returned the money he stole, she would be set free.

They arrived at their location, a condo in a cul-de-sac at the top of Santa Rosalia. The other condos were sparsely occupied, so there wasn't much risk of a nosey neighbor getting into their business. They unloaded Lupe, and Uncle Tommy led her towards one of the two bedrooms.

Mike had arrived before them, and he looked in disbelief when they walked passed him with Lupe. After Uncle Tommy parked her in the bedroom, he returned to where Mike was sitting on a bar stool.

"No one is gonna take a mutha fucking thing from us," Uncle Tommy said and Uncle Mike nodded his head in agreement. Mike said Dave was on his way, and when he arrived we will let Jorge know that we have one of his prized possessions.

They were all sitting around, the TV watching them when Dave came through the door. Mike filled him in on the current state of affairs.

"You have his woman; how did you do that?" Dave asked, sounding like this was unbelievable.

Mike assured him that they in fact did have her, but Dave had to go see for himself. When he returned, Mike told him to call Jorge. He did and passed Mike the phone.

Jorge's voice went into an instant shouting storm as soon as he identified the calling party. "I will kill all of you!" His Spanish accent heavy as he actually had the nerve to curse and threaten them after stealing their money.

Mike tried to talk commonsense to Jorge but that didn't seem to be working, he said,

"Get our money back to us if you ever want to see Lupe again!" Then hung up.

"What do we do now?" Dave asked.

"We keep her until we get our money back," Tommy said.

"You think he's just going to come over here and hand over our money? I've seen you in action, he would be a dead man."

Tommy shaking his head in agreement, said, "I don't know. He can meet us somewhere in a public place and give the money back. Either that or he'll lose his woman."

Dave's face looked real concerned over that statement. He knew Tommy was deadly serious.

For the next three days, no word from Jorge. The Lils: Lil Mike, Lil Ant, and Lil Larry, babysat Lupe. And Uncle Mike and Uncle Tommy made sure she was unharmed. This was merely a money retrieving operation.

Uncle Tommy made sure food was made available to her every day, and he even bought her some clean undies to wear. When he brought the clean undies to her, he was caught off guard when she advanced. "I would love to be with you."

Uncle Tommy could only shake his head. What an impossible spot Jorge had left his woman in. Although she looked very sexy, he could see in her eyes that she knew she needed to do something desperate to save her life. She knew better than them that her man wasn't coming to her rescue.

Uncle Tommy declined her offer, and promptly exited the room. *Poor lady.* She had and would suffer because of Jorge's wrong choice, an unethical business practice.

Jorge's failure to bring back the stolen money within three days placed his wife in a perilous situation. Faced with this predicament, the three men convened to discuss their course of action. Mike and Tommy, driven by anger and a desire for retribution, believed that Lupe should bear the consequences of her husband's wrongdoing.

Dave, known for his tact and negotiation skills, intervened, his strategic thinking and resourcefulness always guiding him. With a calm demeanor, he assured the men that he would personally retrieve the money. Amidst tense emotions and uncertainty, Dave's charisma and diplomacy managed to assuage the others. His promise to recover the stolen funds was received with reluctance but yet received. He took Lupe to make sure nothing happen to her in the course of his negotiations.

This path would lead them to unexpected alliances, unmask hidden truths, a journey that would change their lives forever and ultimately determine their fate and their own intertwined destinies.

Dave would return with the money later that night. And the crew had gained a loyal subject, Lupe. She admired how they handled the situation, even how they snatched her up so quickly after her husband's transgressions. It was her family that held the keys to a warehouse of cocaine, not Jorge's. And she vowed to do all she could to make their crew wealthier.

DAVE'S APPETITE

Love is never any better than the lover. Wicked people love wickedly, violent people love violently, weak people love weakly, stupid people love stupidly, but the love of a free man is never safe. There is no gift for the beloved. The lover alone possesses the gift of love. The loved one is shorn, neutralized, frozen in the glare of the lover's inward eye. Toni Morrison

Love is never any better than the lover, a truer statement about the state of a love affair has never been uttered.

Dad having so many of what we call "Baddies" today, I would say is proof positive of his lover boy status. By many, dad's love was described as passionate. One friend said, he loved every woman that he was ever with. He treated them all with the utmost respect, never talking foul to them, and he always showed whichever one he was with for the moment, a great time.

Men like him are hard to understand and often misunderstood. But as his friend said, dad had a lot of love to go around, and he wanted to share it with numerous women. His love, although many women may disagree, was only the genuine gift of the beloved.

As often as my dad's friends told me how great a spirit he had and how big a heart he had, in their very next sentence they would tell me how much of a playboy he was.

The women he entered into relationships with never complained about cruelty, any poor manners, or even a bad day. All of them only said that he was very loving. And they wanted to possess that great love all for themselves, thus their only source of disappointment. Getting David Harris to commit to one woman was ultimately impossible. Dad was spreading it around.

Playing around was his modus operandi and was as legendary as his street diplomacy. Hugh Hefner was a celebrated playboy known worldwide, and its rumored that dad slept with more women. He had an extremely high body count.

My father's mating hanky-panky left such a big riff between the three mothers of his children that the children suffered. My oldest brother, Davon by Donna and my middle sister, Britney by Karen, and me and my younger brother, Donovan would be greatly affected.

Britney and I would eventually make a pact. But Davon and I never really bonded. Before my grandmother, Fannie, died, she told me something and made me swear to keep it a secret, so I can never divulge it. But she did make a point to let me know how much dad wanted his children to have a bond with one another.

Love affairs can be a tangled web of emotions, desires, and sometimes, unintended consequences. In the case of my dad, David Harris Sr., his charismatic presence and allure seemed to attract women who went to extraordinary lengths to be with him. While I choose to withhold specific names out of respect for their privacy, their stories shed light on the complexities of relationships and the impact they have on the lives of all involved.

Uncle Terry, always a reliable source of wisdom, shared insights into my dad's character and the dynamics of these relationships. He made it clear that my father never encouraged or sought out any kind of violent behavior toward another. Instead, the violence inflicted in this case, was the result of some woman's misguided thoughts and unrealistic viewpoints.

One particular situation deteriorated to the extent that it reached a dangerous and tragic climax. One of the women that dad had previously been involved with, consumed by anger resorted to a violent act. In a fit of rage, she fired a bullet through the door of his house, unintentionally injuring the woman who happened to be in his company at that unlucky moment.

The consequences of my father's actions had spiraled out of control, causing pain and harm to those involved. It's clear evidence of the destructive power of infidelity and the collateral damage it can inflict on innocent lives.

This woman, consumed by her love for my dad, resorted to an extreme measure, resulting in the loss of another woman's limb, forever altering the lives of those involved. The gravity of this event serves as a reminder of the intensity and unpredictability of human emotions. It highlights the lengths to which some individuals may go when caught up in the throes of obsession and unchecked passion – a distorted and misguided version of love.

Terry emphasized that my father was not responsible for the actions of others. He was unwittingly caught in the crosshairs of someone else's unhealthy fixation. This is a painful reminder that even the most charismatic and well-intentioned individuals can find themselves in the midst of destructive situations.

This story illustrates the impactful affect my father's sway had on certain individuals. His charm, charisma, and magnetism elicited intense emotions in women who encountered him. While my dad may not have actively sought out these relationships, the influence he had on these women's lives cannot be denied.

The complexities of multifaceted relationships can lead to unintended consequences. They can bring both joy and heartache, passion and obsession. This incident and many like it should serve as a wake-up call, highlighting that everyone should approach an intimate relationship with empathy, understanding, and a recognition of the boundaries that should be respected.

As thorough as dad was in other areas of his life, from hearing these disheartening stories, he was not always responsible with the unchecked power he held with women. For me, this underscores the importance of treating others with respect, honesty, and compassion. This is a cautionary tale that taught me to be mindful of the inherent vulnerabilities and complexities of human connections.

As I delve into the story of my father, it is essential to acknowledge the impact he had on the lives of those around him, particularly the women who were drawn to him but to also highlight discrepancies that we all can learn from. His experiences shed light on the intricate dynamics of relationships and the depths to which love, obsession, and misguided intentions can take us.

Moving forward, I carry these lessons with me, understanding that relationships should be nurtured with care, respect, and open communication. And as I captain my own journey, I am reminded of the power of empathy and the importance of recognizing the complexities of love and the human heart.

But dad wasn't the first man that possessed a playboy spirit, nor the last. Plenty of men have been more notorious than he, even celebrated. Hugh Heffner maintained a Beverly Hills mansion full of hotties that entertained his guest in an elaborate world of debauchery which included famous movie stars and recording artists. Parties filled with half naked young women in bunny costumes, was the talk of the city. He published a magazine to highlight his exploits and later a television show was produced to reveal to the world Hugh's risqué lifestyle.

Even in our sophisticated world today, some women still find themselves ensnared by the allure of a playboy personality, believing they can be the one to tame his wildness. However, I question whether any woman could truly subdue the magnificent spirit that David Harris possessed. It was a force too powerful for any single individual, even too immense for this entire world. Perhaps that's why he transitioned so early, to find a place that could better contain and appreciate his dynamic personality, where his exuberance and charisma would find a suitable stage to shine upon.

VERN

In my quest to know all I could know about the man that birthed me, I came across people like Vernon Mabins. Vernon, called Vern, by most, shared with me his relationship with my father and his great appreciation for him and how dad helped improve his life.

"I had never in my life met a guy like David Harris. His calm demeanor was the first thing that attracted me to him, causing me to also desire a calm demeanor. Although at the time, my Lion would occasionally roar. But Dave consistently took the high road. He was a remarkable individual.

In the 1980s, I had the privilege of owning Nationwide Pager Company, a prominent business in the Los Angeles area during the era when pagers reigned supreme as the cutting-edge communication technology long before text messaging was on the scene. My company catered to an exclusive clientele, particularly the city's top hustlers, who relied on pagers to stay connected and ahead of the game. Dave was among my first customers.

Dave was known for his unparalleled lifestyle as he consistently sought out the finest luxuries, from flaunting brand-new Ferraris to residing in lavish mansions nestled in the hills. He effortlessly attracted the most stunning women in the city, making him a figure of admiration and envy in our community.

Seeing Dave's success, left an impressible mark on my entrepreneurial journey, as I witnessed the powerful allure and impact he had on even the lives of Hollywood stars. At the forefront of your dad success and influence, he owned a beauty salon in Hollywood. I forget the name of it but when he took me with him to visit it one day, I was impressed to see his star-studded clientele. At that moment, I knew I needed to legitimize myself.

Although many famous singers and actors sought after our drug, some were our best customers, Dave commanded people that weren't hooked on coke. And he fit perfectly in the Hollywood scene with his movie star personality.

David had an aura unlike any I had ever witnessed and unlike none I have seen since he died. Something about him attracted people to him, that made you want to be around him. It wasn't just his physical presence, although he was undeniably handsome with his striking features and confident stance. It was an intangible quality that emanated from within him, an energy that drew others in.

When he walked into a room, all eyes turned toward him. It was as if a magnetic force field surrounded him, capturing the attention and curiosity of everyone present. People gravitated towards him, eager to engage in conversation, seek advice, or simply bask in the warmth of his company. He had a natural charisma that was impossible to ignore.

But it wasn't just his charisma that made him special. David was a great leader, not in the traditional sense of commanding authority or ruling over others, but in the way that he inspired and uplifted those around him. He had a genuine interest in people and their well-being, and he always took the time to listen and offer guidance when needed.

I'm glad that I was one of the people he took under his wing. As a young man navigating the cold streets, I was easily swayed and I didn't understand how vulnerable I was to the temptations and dangers that lurked around every corner. I don't think that many of us actually did, except David. He became my mentor, teaching me valuable life lessons and showing me how to conduct myself in a way that would keep me out of harm's way.

He taught me about the importance of integrity and maintaining a strong image, even when faced with difficult choices. He instilled in me a sense of self-respect and encouraged me to pursue my dreams, no matter how impossible they seemed. David believed in the power of perseverance and hard work, and he led by example, showing me that success was within reach if I was willing to put in the effort.

But it wasn't all serious life lessons with David. He knew how to enjoy life to the fullest and find joy in the simplest of things. One of my favorite moments with him was our occasional trips to Las Vegas on Friday evenings. We would indulge in the exciting world of gambling, trying our luck on the dice table. And when it came to dining, David had a knack for finding the best five-star restaurants where we would savor exquisite meals.

Amidst the joy and laughter, we shared, tragedy struck, and my world was shattered, the entire community of hustlers' world was shook. It felt like the entire world had come to a standstill. I couldn't bring myself to believe the news when I heard that David had drowned. It seemed inconceivable that someone so full of life, so vibrant and invincible, could be taken away so suddenly.

In that moment, I experienced a wave of emotions that I had never encountered before. Grief washed over me like a tidal wave, consuming my every thought and leaving me broken down in tears. I clung to the hope that it was all a terrible mistake, a cruel joke, but deep down, I knew it was true. I had lost my friend and my mentor.

David had always told me to be strong, to show no weakness in the face of adversity. But on that day, as the tears streamed down my face, I couldn't help but feel utterly helpless. The loss of such a beloved figure in my life was a blow that struck at the very core of my being and it questioned everything I thought I knew about strength and resilience. How could I be strong when someone I admired and loved had been taken away so abruptly?

In the days that followed, I found myself in daze. I struggled to come to terms with the reality of David's absence, struggling with an overwhelming sense of emptiness that seemed impossible to fill. Memories of our time together flooded my mind, both comforting and torturous at the same time. I longed for his guidance, his wisdom, and his infectious chuckle that could brighten even the worst days.

But amidst the pain, I realized that David's impact on my life was far from over. His teachings, his words of wisdom, and the examples he set for me were etched deeply into my soul. I had the privilege of knowing him, of experiencing the uncanny effect he had on those around him, and I knew that I had to honor his memory by carrying forward the lessons he had imparted to me.

Dave showed me that life could be unpredictable and cruel, but it was how we responded to those challenges that defined us. As I began to properly deal with my loss, I embraced my vulnerability, and allowed myself to grieve and process the pain, but I didn't let it consume me entirely, although the pain attempted to smother me.

I had learned from David how to be resilient and as I began to reflect on the incredible impact he had on others, I understood my way forward. The way David effortlessly drew people in, the way he inspired them to be better versions of themselves, I would now do my best to immolate that type of personality.

I realized that his legacy was not confined to his physical presence but lived on through the lives he had touched. I made a vow to myself that I would strive to embody the qualities he possessed and continue his work of making a positive difference in the lives of others.

Though he was no longer physically present, I felt his presence in the lessons he had taught me. I could almost hear his voice guiding me, urging me to be strong, to persevere, and to continue living life to the fullest. It wasn't an easy journey, the pain of his loss lingering. And there were moments when I felt overwhelmed by the weight of it all but every time that empty feeling arose, I drew strength from the memories we shared, from the laughter and joy we experienced together.

As time passed, the rawness of the grief began to subside, replaced by a deep sense of gratitude for having known David Harris. I realized that his impact on my life went beyond the moments we spent together. His teachings had become a part of me, shaping my character and influencing the choices I made. I carried his legacy with me, becoming a living example of the awesome effect he had on my life.

In the years that followed, I sought opportunities to mentor others, to lend a helping hand, and to be a source of inspiration and guidance, just as he had been for me. I channeled my grief into a driving force to make a positive impact, to uplift those around me, and to carry forward the lessons he had taught me.

David's physical presence may have faded from this world, but his spirit lives on through the lives he touched. His legacy lives on, guiding me through rough times and reminding me that even in the face of loss, love and inspiration can endure.

Along my journey, I've encountered countless individuals whose lives had been touched by him. And without fail, everyone always agree that Dave was an all-around good dude. Stories of his kindness, his wisdom, and his unwavering belief in the potential of others echoed through the hearts of those he had impacted as confirmation of the indelible mark he had left on this world.

Inspired by these stories, I realized that David's legacy extended far beyond my own personal experiences. He had touched the lives of so many, and it was my responsibility to ensure that his influence continued to ripple outward. I sought out even more opportunities to share his teachings, to pass on the wisdom he had imparted to me, and to keep his memory alive in the hearts and minds of others.

I saw firsthand the transformative power as I witnessed individuals finding strength, overcoming obstacles, and embracing their own potential. It was as if David's spirit lived on through each person he had touched, continuing to inspire and uplift long after he was gone.

But amidst the joy and fulfillment that came from carrying forward David's legacy, remained moments of sorrow and longing. I couldn't help but wonder what life would be like if he were still here. What new lessons and experiences we could have shared, what more he could have accomplished, and the impact he could have continued to make on the world. The void his absence left behind is a reminder of how short life can be and the importance of cherishing the moments we have with those we love.

In my moments of reflection, I find solace in the fact that I was blessed to have known such a person on my visit to earth. As long as I have air in my lungs, I will count my time with your father as timeless treasures.

With time, the pain of my loss transformed into bittersweet gratitude. Gratitude for having known David and glad that I had come to understand that his physical departure was not an end but a new beginning, a call to action for me to embody the qualities he embodied and to make a positive impact in my own unique way.

I continue to live my life guided by the lessons of resilience, integrity, and compassion. I strive to be a light in the lives of others. While I will forever miss my friend's physical presence, I find comfort in knowing that the essence of David lives on, not only in my heart but in all the other hearts touched by his remarkable aura.

David's life and untimely passing taught me a valuable lesson about the fleeting nature of existence, constantly reminding me to cherish each moment, to embrace the connections I make, and to strive to leave a positive imprint on this earth, making this world a better place than I found. For it is in these actions that we create a legacy that transcends time, allowing our spirit to endure long after we are gone."

DETROIT

Uncle Deucy, my father's closest confidant, told me so many stories about their life together that when all are told, will fill up a trilogy. Although, many things he told me was extremely personal and will never be recorded, but I hoped those have shared and will share have entertained while causing you to think about your own life and existence.

Deucy shared with me the time that law enforcement was all over them, and my dad was able to slip through their grasp, which had become an exercise they would have to rinse and repeated often during those times. The government had tasked the FBI and DEA with stemming the rushing tide of drugs in this country.

Deucy said, "It was time for the family to make another move, one more drastic than all the previous ones. Key players in our organization were getting busted or venturing off to do their own thing and LA had become too small with our names ringing on every street corner."

When one of the eighteen wheelers from their trucking company was busted leaving Miami, the wheels were quickly set in motion to get out of town. It was time for a change of scenery. This move had to happen probably quicker than many had anticipated, but now it was imperative if they wanted to remain free from prosecution.

Dad set his sights on Detroit, a city known for its thriving underworld culture. He had visited here numerous times, and had enjoyed immensely. It was a place where the product my father sold, cocaine, held a strong allure for its inhabitants. He had even set up a small operation there but now he would make Detroit his home away from home.

This move carried with it many implications and unknowns. Detroit had been known as a mob city for years, having a well-established mob structure. And outsiders weren't commonly welcomed. But David's charm seemed to hypnotize them. And the prices he could sell cocaine to the home-grown dealers were well below the current price they were paying.

It didn't take long before the dealers at the top of the food chain to begin to hate him. The low LA prices that dad could sell his product couldn't be matched by the local dealers, so before long he was serving most of their clientele. And Detroit began to create challenges.

Despite, the fact that he had become a target of the native sons of Detroit, the winters were brutal, especially for a southern California guy. And he also wrestled with getting his product across the 2,300-mile distance between Los Angeles and his new environs. Meanwhile, the stash spots designed into the interior of automobiles would have to work.

Dave was busy getting his living conditions properly established. Deucy helped him get moved into his new house in Southfield, an up and coming community for prominent businessmen in Detroit. And Deucy would also lend a hand in getting his car dealership set up, a front for his operation.

Detroit proved to be a fertile ground for my father's business ventures. After a month in Detroit, Dave told Deucy, "We're gonna be richer in six months than we have been in the whole five years we've been selling drugs in LA."

He quickly established a reputation as a charming businessman, capitalizing on the demand for his product. And he eventually came up with an ingenious way to get his product the 2300 miles. He hired Charter buses, and gave poor people a free vacation to Detroit with a two hundred dollar a day per diem. Amongst the visitor's luggage was tons of cocaine.

One day as they were sitting around the house, Deucy said, "Man, this is a different world out here, these niggas really get dressed up."

Without hesitation, dad said, "Let's go shopping. And we gotta get you a warm coat too." Dad took Deucy to City Slickers, the store that all the Detroit hustlers and players, major or minor, shopped.

The store's owner recognized my father as soon as he walked through the door. "What can I help you with today, Mr. Harris?"

"We need to introduce my brother Deucy to Detroit styles."

"Right this way, this is where my special clients like your brother Dave shops Deucy," the owner said. The men followed him to a room full of suits. "These are Brioni suits, the suits fine material will just drape over your body. What are you about a 52?" as he took a suit jacket from a rack and helped Deucy into it.

"We'll take it and six more like it. Do you sell mink coats here too?" Dave asked.

"From the best designers, Dennis Basso and Oscar de la Renta. Right over here."

He escorted them into another room, full of mink coats. Deucy touched the material and smiled.

That night, Dave and Deucy were in the front row at Joe Louis Arena, listening to Pattie LaBelle's exquisite voice. Dave caught this pretty young woman staring at him and as soon as he winked, she smiled a radiant smile and winked back, I knew your dad would be taking her home with him that night, Deucy said.

Deucy told me a few days later that law enforcement confiscated a bus loaded with 500 kilos and they quickly fill up another bus load, which arrived three days later. Imagine losing, ten million dollars and spending another ten million the next minute.

When dad and Deucy flew back to LA, Deucy said he loved to go get a burger from Fatburger. They would drive through the city to the Fatburger in Beverly Hills. "Let's go get a Fatburger. I haven't had one since the Reseda Skating Rink days," Deucy said, saying it as my dad would. Dad enjoyed their burgers so much that he planned to one day buy the franchise.

While dad was back in LA, he would always find the time to climb aboard a horse and gallop out in the wide-open countryside. He found something so refreshing about the sheer power of speed. But a horse charging forward at his command with the breeze blowing in his face, was some of his happiest moments.

When he was in Detroit, his mansion was a place where he entertained guests and reveled in the opulence that his lifestyle afforded him. And his car lot was soon catering to the desires of Detroit's elite. Dad had an eye for luxury and knew precisely what the city's bourgeoisie desired and his business thrived.

With success in the drug game, comes danger. And my father's rise in the criminal underworld did not go unnoticed. Rival crews, envious of his wealth and influence, began to plot his downfall. Detroit was a city fueled by competition, where power struggles played out in the shadows and with gunfire in broad open daylight. The threat of violence hung in the air, as rival factions vied for control of the lucrative drug trade.

But amidst this dangerous dance, my father never stopped being a playboy. It was just in his blood. His charisma as well as his extravagant lifestyle would be sufficient in attracting the attention of Detroit's most sought-after females. He reveled in the company of beautiful women, his reputation as a ladies' man preceding him wherever he went. But he knew these carnal alliances could be risky, as jealousy and betrayal lurked around every corner.

One particular conquest, a woman who had fallen for my father's charm, found herself torn between her affection for him and her loyalty to a rival crew. She knew of the plot to end my father's life, a secret that could cost her everything, even her life. But in a brave act of defiance, she risked her own safety and revealed the impending danger to my father.

She said that the gang leaders hated them in Detroit because they were not only encroaching but owning their territory. Dave was grateful to be informed, this revelation setting his wheels in motion. He had been oblivious to the brewing storm, unaware of the danger that loomed over his head. The woman's act of courage highlighted the complexities of my father's life in Detroit – a world where loyalty and betrayal coexisted.

Detroit, a city where dreams were shattered and lives were forever changed, a playground and a battlefield, Dave would wade through the treacherous landscape in his usual carefree manner. But this city constantly served a harsh reminder of the price one paid when engaging in a world fueled by greed, power, and desperation. The murder rate associated with drug-deals-gone-wrong was soaring.

My father, ever vigilant, took immediate action to protect himself. He moved to another home, not giving anyone except Deucy and Uncle Mike the address, so he could live more of secluded life. He increased security measures, surrounded himself with trusted allies, and prepared for the inevitable confrontation. The threat of violence became a constant companion, hovering over their lives like an ominous cloud.

As tensions escalated, the city of Detroit became a powder keg ready to explode. In the midst of this chaos, my father's survival instincts kicked into high gear. He maneuvered in the deadly terrain of Detroit's criminal underworld, always one step ahead of his enemies. The street smarts and cunningness that he had perfected, allowed him to outmaneuver his rivals, securing his place in a vicious game.

But the stakes continued to rise, and the tension in Detroit reached its breaking point. The rival crews were determined to eliminate my father, viewing him as a threat that needed to be eradicated. Their plots grew more sinister, their methods more ruthless.

Amidst this escalating danger, the woman who had risked her own life to warn my father found herself caught in the crossfire. She became a pawn in the deadly game, her loyalty to my father and her betrayal of her own crew putting her in grave danger. As the rival factions closed in, my father made a difficult decision to protect her, arranging for her to leave Detroit and start a new life far away from all of the chaos.

He prioritized her safety over his own desires, acknowledging the sacrifices she had made and the risks she had taken to save his life. The complex web of relationships that entangled my father's life, where love and danger coexisted in an intricate waltz, became an ordinary day in the life and times of David Harris.

In his efforts to outmaneuver his enemies, he sought more allies within Detroit's criminal underworld, employing strategic maneuvers and exploiting his enemies' weaknesses. He formed tenuous partnerships, alliances built on mutual self-interest. But in the drug game, loyalties could shift like the changing of socks.

When things really heated up, dad would always escape to the safety of Los Angeles. And on one of those occasions, he bought a house in Encino on Hayvenhurst not far from Michael Jackson's Encino estate.

BOATING ACCIDENT

There was a report that the FBI and DEA was investigating and on the verge of getting an indictment against David Harris, a reputed drug lord. In his carefree style, Dave didn't put too much stock in law enforcement investigations into his criminal matters. He felt that he had successfully shielded himself by using buffers to do the heavy lifting in his operations. He would only collect the money in a number of secret stash houses.

For Memorial Day 1988, Dave and the four men in his party had breakfast at a quaint little restaurant on Catalina, then he met a few of his friends on the water in his boat. His friends, Freeway Rick and Rodney, were already on the water in their boats.

After breakfast, Dave and his entourage zoomed in his boats through the smooth waters, out to where the other were. Everyone were having a spectacular time and enjoying a beautiful day. Many people had brought their boats out for the holiday.

The wind felt different across a face as a boat flew into it. Occasionally, Dave would throttle down, pulling his boat up next to a boat full of women. Once he secured the promise of a date or a phone number from the woman he was in pursuit of, he would point his boat into the wind again.

Right before noon, the clear blue sky turned dark and angry, and the wind began swirling. A coast guard boat cruised through the water, a guard shouting, "Wind Advisory, get your boats to shore!" Their lovely outing had quickly turned into something harrowing as the approaching clouds looked dark and mean.

The daredevil in Dave reluctantly turned back after consistent encouragement from the men on his boat, some of them even pleading. When he wheeled the boat back toward the shore, it stalled. He tried to get the engine to turn over again, but it wouldn't. He went below to see if he could manually get it to turn over.

After a few minutes, the swirling winds setting the boat adrift, Deucy followed Dave's path into the engine room. The howling wind and crashing waves made it difficult to maintain his footing, but his concern for his friend propelled him forward.

As Deucy descended into the engine room, the sight that greeted him was even more distressing than he had imagined. It was a chaotic scene. Water gushed in from multiple openings, filling the compartment rapidly. He didn't see Dave. "Dave!" Deucy shouted over the deafening noise, his voice barely audible.

A few seconds later, Dave's head popped up from beneath the water, his face reflecting a mix of fear and determination as he spotted Deucy. "Deucy, help! My leg is trapped," he yelled, his voice strained.

Deucy waded through the murky water, fighting against the force of the swelling tide that was up to his chest. With every step, the urgency to save his friend grew. He reached Dave and bobbed under the water to see what held him captive and saw wiring wrapped around his leg. Deucy tried to untangle him but couldn't. Running out of oxygen, he came up for air. Then went right back under, he yanked at the wires but couldn't get his friend free.

He popped up for air, and dipped under again, desperately struggling to help Dave free himself from the wiring that held him captive. But not being accustomed to holding his breath for long periods, Deucy was forced to come up for air often.

Deucy went under a third time, refusing to give up. He knew he couldn't leave his friend behind. The water level continued to rise, now reaching their chests, making their task even more challenging.

Time seemed to stretch as Deucy and Dave battled against the rising water and the entrapment. The boat groaned under the strain of the raging sea, adding to the sense of impending doom. Deucy's hands trembled as he fumbled with the knots, his mind racing for a solution.

Suddenly, a loud crack reverberated through the air, and the boat lurched violently. Deucy's heart sank as he realized their situation had become even more dire. Panic surged through his veins, urging him to act swiftly.

Deucy came up for air, and shouted, "The boat is sinking!" His voice filled with desperation.

Dave's eyes widened, his body tensing with a mix of fear and determination. "Go, get help!"

Deucy's eyes welled up with tears, torn between his loyalty to Dave and the reality of their predicament. Reluctantly, he made a split-second decision. Knowing time was running out, he turned and raced towards the nearest exit, praying that help would arrive in time for his friend.

As Deucy rushed through the water, each step heavier than the next, he reached the steps and turned back, seeing Dave drifting. He burst onto the main deck, meeting a somber sight. The other passengers had abandoned the sinking boat, seeking refuge on nearby vessels that had responded. Desperation washed over Deucy as he realized he was the last one left on Dave's boat.

Frantically, Deucy pleaded with the rescuers, his voice filled with anguish. "Please, you have to help! Dave is still trapped below deck! He needs help!"

The rescue teams immediately sprang into action, their training and experience guiding their every move. They directed their focus towards Dave's boat, determined to save him from the clutches of the sinking vessel. Two coast guards came aboard and one of them quickly helped Deucy get into a life jacket, then tossed him into the turbulent waters where other rescuers helped him unto the rescue boat.

Deucy stood on the deck of the rescue boat, his heart heavy with grief and disbelief. But as time ticked away, hope began to fade. Despite their valiant efforts, the rescue teams were unable to reach Dave in time and jumped to save themselves.

The sinking boat took Dave, Deucy's loyal friend, down with it. Tears streamed down Deucy's face as he struggled to come to terms with this devastating reality. The boat's descent into the depths of the ocean, left behind a sense of loss that would forever haunt Deucy.

The surrounding boats fell into a solemn silence, their engines idling as a mark of respect for the fallen. The once joyous atmosphere had transformed into somber disbelief for all that were present.

Deucy's mind was a mix of emotions and guilt for leaving Dave behind. Sorrow rushed over him and he shook inconsolable as he felt a deep sense of helplessness. He clenched his fists, fighting against the overwhelming despair threatening to consume him.

In the midst of his grief, a hand gently rested on Deucy's shoulder. It was one of the rescue team members. His face was filled with compassion as he softly said, "We're so sorry for your loss. We did everything we could."

Deucy nodded, his voice choked with sorrow. "Thank you for trying."

As the rescue boat pulled away from the now-sunken vessel, Deucy looked back one last time, etching the memory of Dave and their shared adventures into his heart and he thought he saw Dave back-stroking in the water. But it was an illusion.

Deucy vowed to honor his friend's memory by cherishing the moments they had shared as the boat sped away. Days turned into weeks, and the weight of grief never lessened. Deucy felt empty and dead inside.

He tried to find solace in the support of their friends. And as he tried to recall his fondest memories with his brother, too much pain accompanied each memory. He sought professional help, and after months of therapy, nothing change. Deucy knew his life would never be the same ever again.

He was debilitated from the tragic event. He found himself visiting numerous psychiatrists. Each doctor would encourage Deucy in their own way to treasure each moment he and his friend had together. One doctor would tell him things like "the enduring power of the friendship that the two of you enjoyed transcends death," as she tried to help him find some comfort.

Only the fact that Dave would want him to carry on, got him moving toward a sense of normalcy again. As he attempted to find joy in life once more, he would often break down in tears as he thought about never having Dave beside him ever again.

Deucy began to hold on dearly to his deep appreciation for the precious moments that were gifted to him with his friend, his brother. He never failed to share stories of Dave's bravery and infectious laughter, ensuring his brother's memory lived on.

COUSIN MILTON

Cousin Milton came to live with my father when he was just fifteen years old. My father, being the compassionate man, he was, took him in without hesitation and cared for him as if he were his own younger brother.

Over the years, Milton and my father developed an everlasting bond. They shared a unique connection, participating together in experiences that created a sense of trust and understanding that transcended ordinary familial relationships. Milton knew secrets that no one else did, secrets that were buried deep within my father's heart.

The news of my father's unexpected passing left his friends and family in disbelief. But this news crushed Milton more than anyone, leaving him actually debilitated. How could Dave, who had lived such a carefree and full life, be dead? That just couldn't be true. As everyone wrestled to find their peace with the thought of his loss in their own way, Milton couldn't.

Shortly after my father's death, Milton was kidnapped by unknown assailants. They wanted to know where my father had hidden his millions. A heartless act, fueled by greed and desperation, taking an already distraught Milton through a frightening ordeal.

For hours, Milton endured physical and psychological torture, as they tried to extract any information he might have about the whereabouts of the hidden fortune. But Milton, loyal to the core, remained steadfast, refusing to betray my father's trust, even if it meant his own death.

Eventually, his captors released him, realizing that their efforts were in vain. But the trauma Milton had endured damaged his soul. He withdrew from the world, retreating into a self-imposed seclusion. The weight of what he had been through was too heavy to bear, and he struggled to find his peace again in the wake of such darkness.

The scars left by that harrowing experience were more than physical, his psyche was shocked almost beyond repair. Milton's voice quivered, and tears streamed down his face as he recalled the anguish that still haunted him after nearly three decades.

This experience, along with the loss of Dave, his beloved older cousin turned big brother, had left a wound that time had failed to heal, a wound that continued to seep pain and sorrow.

It was during this interview that Milton's emotions overwhelmed him and he was able to let it all out, probably for the first time. Just mentioning my father's name, would get him all choked up. His love for my father was deep, and the void left by his passing was immeasurable. The pain he carried within him was a confirmation to the depth of their connection, a bond forged through shared experiences and unwavering loyalty.

Although his life had taken a dark turn in this cruel twist of fate, the ruthless assailants were unable to break Milton. The mere thought of Milton facing death's cold stare sent shivers down my spine.

Despite the trauma, Milton cherished the memories they had created together and held them close to his heart. In his tears, I saw a reflection of the love and loss that we all felt, a reminder of how impactful my father had been on those around him. Milton's tears and his unwavering loyalty ignited a fire within me – a fire that would lead me to the heart of my father's story, to the hidden secrets of his life.

In the years that followed my father's death, Milton found comfort in the memories of his time with my father, adoring them like precious treasures. His love for my father served as a source of strength and inspiration. Milton's story serves as a testament to the enduring power of love and strength.

During this very emotional interview, I couldn't help but be moved by the sheer heartbreak that Milton was still experiencing. Milton had sought therapy to help him process the trauma he had endured, slowly unraveling the layers of pain that had consumed him, a long and arduous road.

As time went on, Milton began to open up to trusted friends and family, sharing his experiences. Through these conversations, he found solace in knowing that his emotions were valid and that others understood the magnitude of his loss. The support he received from loved ones helped him rebuild his shattered spirit and find renewed purpose.

Cousin Milton said when the thought of how he and my father loved each other, was what pushed him forward and motivated him. To honor my father's memory, he created a successful life for himself, working diligently, determined to reclaim his life. With a newfound sense of purpose, Milton poured his energy into his work in the military then as an entrepreneur.

Milton's tears were not just tears of grief; they were tears of gratitude for the meaningful affect my father had on his life. Through his tears, I found not only the pain of loss but also the beauty of a connection that transcends time and the unwavering love that can withstand even the darkest of trials.

In that vulnerable moment, as Milton was laying bare his soul, I was able to witness the depth and magnitude of true love. It was a reminder that love, in its purest form, has the power to transcend time and distance, that true love never dies. Despite the passage of years and the hardships endured, Milton's love helped me to understand more clearer than ever the importance of cherishing those we hold dear.

Although the interview with Cousin Milton was a rollercoaster ride of emotions. It was also an intense experience that left me on the edge of my seat, hanging onto every word that escaped his lips. But Milton's reluctance to open up about certain aspects of his past fueled my curiosity, and I was determined to unearth the truth behind the enigma called David Harris. I didn't want to push him though, so I made a mental note to ask other people that might have this information.

Milton did share other positive aspects of their relationship that he felt were exciting. "When I arrived at your father's doorstep as a wide-eyed fifteen-year-old, little did I know that my life was about to take an exhilarating turn. From the sleepy countryside to the bustling streets of Los Angeles, my world transformed at breakneck speed. I would learn that my love for fast cars and adrenaline-pumping adventures, mirrored your father's. I was like a young bird, spreading its wings for the first time, soaring through the City of Angels in a Ferrari or Porsche at speeds that seemed to defy gravity."

He laughed when he spoke of my dad's speed demon personality. "Wherever he was going, he wasted no time getting there," Milton said, recalling a time when the two of them raced a stretch of the 101 Freeway from Encino to LA. Dad in his Ferrari and Milton in dad's Porsche. "Your dad rarely drove the speed limit. He had a need for speed."

The tale of this race truly captured my imagination. Milton's voice sung as he recounted the heart-pounding race he and my father engaged in. The image of two daredevils zooming through a sunny Los Angeles day, engines roaring as their adrenaline pumped with the high speeds of the cars, was enough to make my heart race in sync with his. Milton admitted that my father emerged victorious, but the thrill of the race left him feeling invincible, as if he had conquered the world.

In the retelling of this event, I couldn't help but be moved by the strength of his spirit. Despite the darkness that had clouded his life, he found the courage to share his story and honor the memory of a man who had meant the world to him – a reminder that even in the face of unspeakable tragedy, love and loyalty can prevail.

In my quest for answers about my father's life, my personal journey of discovery, every revelation held its own significance. As I peeled back the layers of mystery, determined to uncover the hidden truths, Milton's story had given me a glimpse into a world filled with secrets, adventures, and the unbreakable bond between two souls. It was a world that demanded further exploration.

Armed with Milton's account, I delved deeper into the labyrinth of my father's life. I scoured old photographs, dug through dusty boxes filled with forgotten mementos, and reached out to more individuals who had crossed paths with my father during his wild and enigmatic journey. Each revelation brought me closer to understanding the man my father had been and the impact he had on those around him.

The more I uncovered, the more I realized that my father's life was a tapestry woven with threads of peril and excitement. It was a life lived on the edge, embracing the thrill of the unknown. And as the pieces of the puzzle began to fall into place, I couldn't help but wonder about the hidden fortune that had sparked such turmoil in Milton's life. What had my father been involved in? What secrets had he carried to his grave? The questions swirled in my mind, propelling me forward for more answers.

With each step, I seemed to uncover more about my father's clandestine activities. The world he had lived-in was a double-edged sword, offering exhilaration and danger in equal measure. Tales of high-stakes races, clandestine dealings, and a network of individuals who operated in the shadows. The dark underbelly of my father's world was a realm of risk and intrigue, where trust was a rare commodity, and loyalty was tested at every turn.

Milton's kidnapping was just a glimpse into the treacherous path my father had walked. The assailants had sought his hidden fortune, a fortune that seemed to hold the key to a world of power and influence. But Milton's unwavering loyalty had foiled their plans to get their hands on my father's wealth.

As the mysteries unraveled, I couldn't help but feel a sense of awe. A man yet 26 that had accomplished so much in a world where one wrong move could have dire consequences. And yet, amidst the chaos, he had an unmatched zest for life.

With Milton's blessing and his unwavering support, I ventured further into the mysteries. I sought out individuals who had crossed paths with him, people who had glimpsed the depths of his wild spirit.

I have encountered a cast of characters as diverse as the city itself. There were former associates with their own agendas, reluctant people who carried secrets like burdens – secrets that would never be uttered again. The more I delved, the more I realized that my father's life had left a complex web of relationships, both forged in loyalty and tainted by betrayal. Each encounter brought me closer to the truth, but it also exposed me to a reality I hadn't thoroughly considered – that there might be someone out there that didn't want me to know what really happened that day on the boat.

Even after hearing all of the interviewees, it was still amazing to witness the tremendous magnitude my father had on those around him. His charisma had drawn people to him like moths to a flame, and his larger-than-life persona had left an indelible mark on their lives.

As I followed the breadcrumbs left behind from my father's past, my quest became a search for closure, for understanding, and for a sense of peace. I knew that unraveling the mysteries of his would not only bring closer but would also provide an opportunity for my healing and growth.

Along the way, I faced my own share of challenges. The shadows of my father's world threatened to consume me, and at times, I questioned whether I was prepared for the truth I sought.

As the journey progressed, I discovered that his legacy was more than just a hidden fortune. It was a legacy of resilience, living life in the face of adversity. The stories I uncovered painted a portrait of a man who had danced on the edge of danger, yet had always remained true to his core values.

This truth that I found was not discovered in a hidden vault or a secret stash of wealth, it was found in the connections forged, the lives touched, and the memories that lived on in the hearts of those who had known my father.

I have come to realize that the search for truth was never truly about finding answers – it was about embracing the complexities of life, honoring the legacies of those who had come before me, and discovering my own strength amidst the chaos.

Milton's stories were a catalyst, propelling me into the world that my father inhabited. I am forever grateful for the chance to walk a few steps in his shoes through Cousin Milton and the many others that shared their memories of my father.

MICHAEL RAY HARRIS
AKA HARRY O

There's nothing like living under a lovely LA sunshine. I may be biased because this is my home town, the place where my limbs grew long and strong. But waking up to warm weather on most days, gives me a sense of rejuvenation as I engage in another day.

From the time, my uncle introduced the prospect of working with him in his record business ventures, I responded immediately to the call. I just knew that this was the life for me. And I began to dream.

Out of the four nieces and nephews in our family, including my uncle's daughter, Mykel, I was the only one to answer the bell. As I grew older and learned exactly who my uncle was, I was amazed, and haven't stopped being impressed since that time. It gave me a great sense of pride to know the fame that surrounded his name.

Once he and I was having a conversation while he was still incarcerated and I remember him saying, "Dave and I possessed these unyielding spirits. A flame burned in us that refused to be extinguished."

From a young age, they were taught the value of hard work. Their mother, wise and steadfast, instilled in them the belief that no obstacle was insurmountable and no dream too grand to chase. She nurtured their individual spirits, fostering a relentless pursuit of excellence that became an integral part of their being.

And after spending time with Mamo, I realized where my dad and uncle got their tenacity, their doggedness to be successful. Together, the two men formed an unbreakable bond, a partnership fueled by their shared commitment to escape poverty. Through the highs and lows, they stood side by side, supporting each other through every trial and tribulation. Their combined strength became a force to be reckoned with, an unstoppable tide that surged forward in the face of adversity.

Countless times, they faced setbacks that threatened to shatter their resolve. Yet, like a Phoenix rising from the ashes, they emerged stronger every time. Failure was merely a stepping stone, a lesson learned on the path to success. The men refused to be discouraged, using each stumble as fuel to propel them further towards their goals.

The world around them may have doubted their abilities, casting shadows of uncertainty and skepticism. But they continued marching forward, their unyielding spirit never deterred. They embraced challenges with open arms, relishing the opportunity to prove themselves against all odds.

And through their unwavering dedication, they achieved greatness. Milestones once thought impossible became easy to hurdle along their journey. Their unyielding spirit became the driving force behind their accomplishments, propelling them to reach heights they had only dared to dream of.

On one of my many conversations with Uncle Mike while he was still in prison, I felt so proud to be a Harris when he said, "Me and my brother were cut from a different cloth. We felt like nothing was too big to accomplish." And I knew at that moment, that there was nothing too big for me to accomplish.

I would also understand from Uncle Mike that it wasn't just about the victories. It was about the journey itself – the sweat, the tears, the moments of doubt and fear. It was the process of pushing themselves beyond their perceived limits and discovering the depths of their true potential.

The information that Uncle Mike was sharing with me became an inspiration, reminding me that anything is possible when I refuse to surrender. I learned that within me also lied a flame of determination, waiting to be ignited. I embraced that unyielding spirit, for it was the key that unlocked the doors to unimaginable achievements. I let it guide me through the darkest of times, propelling me towards a future filled with boundless possibilities.

Uncle Tommy and I are working on a TV series called "The Kartier Boys." This series delves into the high-stakes underworld of the 80's as my father and uncle handled the vicious landscape at the height of the illegal drug trade in Los Angeles. This thrilling drama follows their rise to power, their pursuit of legitimacy, and the constant threat of law enforcement hot on their heels. The story revolves around the Harris brothers, Michael and David, who together with their adopted brother Deucy, form the core of their organization. They are joined by a group of cousins hailing from Louisiana and their trusted friend, Big Tommy, a talented collegiate football player. Under the guise of a legitimate limousine company called Kartier Limousine, they establish a thriving drug operation.

For years, the Kartier Boys dominated the Los Angeles drug scene, operating with precision and cunning. However, as their empire expands and law enforcement begins to close in on their illegal activities, they are forced to extend their operations to other major cities such as New York, Detroit, and San Francisco. With the heat intensifying, they find themselves constantly on the edge, always staying one step ahead of the authorities.

As the series unfolds, the Kartier Boys grapple with the desire to transition into legitimate businessmen. Time is running out, and

Michael, the leader of the crew, faces mounting pressures to find an exit strategy from the illicit world they had built.

Along the way, they must handle internal power struggles, external threats, and the constant fear of betrayal. With top members of their organization either facing imprisonment or meeting untimely deaths, the Kartier Boys find themselves in a race against time. They face personal sacrifices, moral dilemmas, and the ever-present danger of their illegal activities catching up with them.

"The Kartier Boys" is a thrilling and intense series that explores themes of family loyalty, ambition, and the consequences of a life of crime. It delves into the complexities of the drug trade, the blurred lines between legality and illegality, and the human desire to win. Through its compelling characters and gripping storylines, the series keeps viewers on the edge of their seats, eagerly anticipating each twist and turn in the Kartier Boys' illicit journey.

I learned from so many people close to their crew, that Uncle Mike had a desire to take the family into prominence. And he knew that black people as a whole was so far behind financially that it would take a century to catch up through conventional means. So, he decided to take the quick route and my dad followed his lead.

With a little early guidance, Uncle Mike could have easily been the CEO of a multi-national corporation. He became the ultimate CEO by his own training but earlier wrong decisions would hinder the enjoyment of his accomplishments.

Uncle Mike was a figure who had been absent from my life for the better part of three decades. The circumstances that led to his prolonged absence were complicated, but despite the physical distance between us, he remained a source of strength and inspiration. Our bond was forged through the occasional 15-minute conversations he managed to have with me from the confines of prison.

During those precious moments, Uncle Mike would impart his wisdom, his experiences, and his unwavering belief in my potential. He saw something in me that I had yet to discover within myself. It was during one of these conversations that the seeds of our creative collaboration were sown.

We decided to start a record company together, which we named Blank Kanvaz. The name came from the belief that everyone starts with a blank canvas and it's up to each individual to paint upon that canvas the life they desire. And the name also symbolized the opportunity for my uncle and I to create something extraordinary, to paint our own masterpiece on the canvas of the music industry. Uncle Mike, with his extensive knowledge of the business and his raw talent as a shrewd businessman, became the guiding force behind our endeavor.

Under Uncle Mike's tutelage, I found myself transforming into a CEO, learning the intricacies of the music industry, and honing my business acumen. He taught me about artist management, contract negotiations, marketing strategies, and the importance of staying ahead of the curve. His unique style and unconventional approach to music left its impression on me, leaving me feeling miles ahead of my counterparts. I realized that to be truly cutting-edge, I had to push boundaries and think outside of the box.

Inspired by Uncle Mike, I began to cultivate other creative ventures. One such endeavor is Legendary Kanvaz, a film company that I founded. With its inception, I sought to merge the worlds of film and music, creating a synergy that will capture the imagination of audiences worldwide.

Legendary Kanvaz is more than just a film company; it is a platform for innovative storytelling and groundbreaking visual experiences. We specialize in producing movies that defy conventions, challenging the traditional norms of filmmaking. Our films are not just stories; they are immersive journeys that push the boundaries of imagination.

We believe that the combination of powerful storytelling and evocative melodies have the potential to create a truly immersive cinematic experience. This unique blend of music and film will become the hallmark of Legendary Kanvaz.

The success of Legendary Kanvaz will be about more than just the films we create, it's also the marketing scheme we have devised to engage with our audience. We recognize that in an increasingly digital and interconnected world, traditional advertising methods are losing their impact. So, we venture into uncharted territory, harnessing the power of social media, viral campaigns, and interactive experiences to create a buzz around our films.

Through the knowledge I gained from Uncle Mike and my own determination, Blank Kanvaz and Legendary Kanvaz will become emboldened symbols of our artistic vision. Our artists are no longer confined by their circumstances or limited by societal expectations. We have taken control of our destinies and are forging our own paths in the creative landscape.

As I reflect upon the journey from those brief phone conversations with Uncle Mike to the establishment of my companies, I am filled with gratitude for his unwavering belief in me. His resilience, his creativity, and his unique perspective on life continue to inspire me every day. Although Uncle Mike was physically absent for much of my life, his influence and guidance has helped shape me into the person I am today.

Together, we have proven that the power of creativity knows no bounds. And as I step into the future, I am determined to carry forward the legacy of David Harris Sr., creating his movie, "Boss Hustla." A film that will resonate, challenge, and leave an impression on the world.

Building on this momentum, we continue to explore diverse genres and narratives. We delve into thought-provoking social dramas, epic fantasy adventures, and even experimental art films that push artistic boundaries. Each project is infused with the spirit of collaboration, as we seek to bring together talented filmmakers, musicians, and artists to create a truly immersive and unforgettable cinematic experience.

Our commitment to pushing creative boundaries extend beyond the films themselves. We establish partnerships with influential artists and organizations to stage innovative marketing campaigns and events. We collaborate with renowned visual artists to create stunning murals that capture the essence of our films, transforming cityscapes into immersive art installations. We organize interactive screenings where audiences can experience the films in unique and unconventional settings, such as rooftop cinemas and underground music venues.

Through these endeavors, Legendary Kanvaz is becoming more than just a film production company; it's becoming a cultural movement. We aim to inspire other artists to break free from traditional molds and embrace their own unique visions. We organize workshops and mentorship programs to support emerging filmmakers and musicians, fostering an environment of creative exploration and collaboration.

As the years passes, the true measure of our success lies in the impact we have on individuals. We have received countless messages from people whose lives have been touched, moved, and even transformed by the stories we tell and the music we create. It is in these moments that we know we have achieved our goal of creating art that resonates deeply with the human experience.

As I reflect on the journey from those 15-minute conversations with Uncle Mike to the establishment of my own company, I'm sincerely grateful for the significant impact his guidance had on my life.

Mogul Maker

One day, I hope to write my uncle's book, which I will call "Mogul Maker: How Harry O Created Death Row Records." It will be an enthralling true story that traces the extraordinary journey of Michael "Harry O" Harris from drug kingpin to music mogul maker.

This tale will follow the remarkable trajectory of Harry O as he strives to transfer his ill-gotten gains into the entertainment industry, faces personal tragedies and legal troubles, and eventually reclaims his place at the helm of one of the most iconic record labels in history.

The story will begin with Harry O and his brother David Harris, along with their associates, amassing wealth and power through their drug empire in Los Angeles. However, Harry O yearns to legitimize his fortune and pursue a new path, which he initially does with a limousine company, and later with Death Row Records.

Checkmate

With Hollywood being only minutes away, Uncle Mike has always had a keen interest in the entertainment world, with looks good enough to even become a movie star himself. He set his sights on that world and initiated the creation of the Broadway play "Checkmates," featuring renowned actors Denzel Washington and Vanessa Bell, his passage into the entertainment world.

Harry O's life takes a dramatic turn when he is arrested for attempted murder, leading to his imprisonment. Then tragedy strikes when David, Harry O's younger brother and partner, tragically drowns in a boating accident, shattering Harry O's world. Amidst the turmoil, he is undeterred by his circumstances, and hatches an audacious plan to launch a Hip-Hop record label from behind bars. Through his sheer determination and resourcefulness, he manages to secure the funding, a substantial sum that propels his vision forward.

Capitalizing on his keen eye for talent, Harry O secures the signing of Dr. Dre, an up and coming producer in the music industry, thus setting the stage for the explosive success of Death Row Records. To manage the label's day to day operations, Harry O's criminal attorney, David Kenner, handpicked Marion "Suge" Knight. However, unbeknownst to Harry O, Kenner's involvement eventually led to betrayal, and to a power struggle that stripped Death Row Records from his control.

Over the years, he faced numerous legal battles and setbacks in his quest to regain his freedom and ownership of his record label. However, a glimmer of hope emerges with the unwavering support of renowned Death Row recording artist, Snoop Dogg.

Together, they embarked on a relentless pursuit of justice and redemption, my uncle determined to reclaim Death Row Records and his freedom. "Mogul Maker" is a gripping tale of ambition, resilience, and the price of success. It delves into the complexities of the music industry, the consequences of personal choices, and the enduring power of the human spirit. Through Harry O's remarkable journey, the story underscores the indomitable will of a man who refuses to be defeated, ultimately triumphing against all odds and reclaiming his freedom.

How impressive is that, a determined soul creates the largest Hip-Hop label in history from a prison cell. Public record will reveal more of who my uncle is than I could ever give you in a few paragraphs.

POSTMORTEM

The weight of the boating accident in 1988 was a heavy burden to bear with far-reaching consequences, as lives were forever altered, and the emotional toll on all those involved underwent. The postmodern period of David Sr.'s life was marked with a sense of disillusionment.

During the research and interview phase of this book, it became apparent that many individuals directly impacted by this event were still too emotionally distraught to fully share their feelings. The trauma and pain endured by loved ones who were incarcerated or affected by the consequences of the boating accident remained raw and unresolved.

Upon his passing, many of his friends and family were in prison and never had the chance to properly mourn their love one and welcome this opportunity. This book serves as the contributor's eulogy, giving them the opportunity to express their fondest memories and heartfelt emotions for the first time in a public forum. In their tributes, these men and women finally got the chance to sing the praises of their dear friend and love one.

Although, the information gathered was often complex, sometimes disheartening but always revealing, I was able to gather what I hope is an entertaining read.

It was complex because dad was a complex person, a person with many layers. But when the layers were peeled back, we found a good ole country boy that loved horseback riding, and having the time of his life in the big city.

My father and uncle Mike had built comfortable lives for themselves in the affluent neighborhood of Encino, Los Angeles. They were transitioning into the life of successful businessmen, known for their entrepreneurial spirit and their involvement in various ventures. However, their success came with a price – a price that would ultimately be paid in the form of losing their homes.

Mayor Tom Bradley, a figure of significant influence and power in governmental affairs, had long been acquainted with my uncle Mike. They had attended social events together, and my uncle had been a familiar face in the circles of Los Angeles' elite. The friendship between the men seemed genuine, built on shared experiences and a mutual understanding.

But beneath the surface of their camaraderie, a different narrative was unfolding. Apparently, some in law enforcement didn't agree with their friendship, and had been gathering information about my father and uncle Mike. Some felt the confiscation was orchestrated by men who held immense power within the city. And after my uncle's arrest for attempted murder, they felt that they had something on the Mayor Bradley and pressured him to act.

One of the most discouraging events that happened after my father's was the confiscation of his and my uncle's homes. In an unprecedented move, Mayor Bradley stepped onto my father's lawn to announce that my father and Uncle Mike were among the largest drug dealers in the United States. The confiscation was aired on Channel 2 evening news.

After Mayor Tom Bradley stood on my father's lawn, announcing that the government was confiscating both of the brother's mansion, FBI and DEA began rounding up dealers all across Los Angeles and in other parts of the country. This event was nothing short of bewildering. Many of my dad's friends said that the Mayor's actions felt like betrayal and the abuse of power.

The confiscation of their homes was carried out with a ruthless efficiency, leaving my family reeling and struggling to comprehend all of it and wondering what was coming next. The family had already lost both men, my uncle was in prison and my father was deceased. So, this came as another devastating blow, both emotionally and financially as family members were trying to recover their love ones' personal possessions.

Years later, as truth began to emerge, whistleblowers and investigative journalists began to uncovered evidence of why so many black and brown men were targeted in selective prosecution scams, and what was really the ulterior motives behind these questionable practices.

It became clear that my father and Uncle Mike had been mere pawns in a game of political maneuvering, their homes seized to serve as a precedence of the new way the government had decided to do business, confiscating the possessions like drug dealers like they did terrorists. And it was done on the news to strike fear in the heart of all the other dealers that would see the new's cycle or hear of it, so they would know what was coming.

EPILOGUE

Senator Biden, now President Biden, was the Democratic floor manager when Congress successfully passed the Comprehensive Drug Laws of 1984 and ten years later in 1994, he was Chairman of the Senate Judiciary Committee, and very strategic in getting the Violent Crime Control and Law Enforcement Act passed through Congress by a majority vote. The Federal government ensured their success across the nation by punishing reluctant states with the threat of not getting Federal subsidies. Big, big mistake, both of them, which Biden would admit while running for the 2020 Presidential election.

The American propaganda machine published a photo of a malnourished, deformed looking baby in a New York newspaper 1986 with the heading "Crack Baby." People cringed, seeing the images of Crack Babies. Even some drug dealers felt guilty over what the drug was doing to babies. Anyone with a soul didn't want to see harm come to a baby.

The "crack baby" image became symbolic with how drug dealers were ruining our society. Crack babies were supposed to create generations of untold expenses, overwhelming school systems and social programs because they wouldn't be able to hold a job or have meaningful relationships.

"The exposure to crack would interfere with the central core of what it is to be human. These babies would become adults, doomed to a life of uncertain suffering, of probable deviance, of permanent inferiority," reports would say.

Crack Babies, children exposed to crack cocaine in utero, children that would be destined to live a life of physical and mental disability. Who were these expert doctors and why did anyone listen to them?

"Less than one percent of babies were affected by their mothers using crack during pregnancy, and of that small percentage, many of those problems were caused because the drug raised the mother's blood pressure, resulting in a premature birth," according to the many new reports provided, twenty-five years later. "Alcohol and tobacco does more damage to the fetus than crack.

Environmental factors like poverty and adverse living conditions where kids are susceptible to seeing someone arrested, hearing gunshots, seeing someone being shot or a dead body results more in the slow development in children, than once being a crack baby. Factors causing depression, anxiety and lower self-esteem should have never been associated with in-utero cocaine exposure."

Poverty has a more powerful influence on the outcome of inner-city children than gestational exposure to cocaine. Why aren't our politicians waging a War on Poverty?

The propagandized information, this lie, helped fashion the sentencing disparity, a primary section of the Anti-Drug Abuse Act of 1986 that Senator Biden helped draft, instituting the 100 to 1 ratio for crack cocaine. Which meant that people convicted of distributing crack would serve an extremely long sentence – one hundred times greater than – the person distributing powder cocaine. Of course, this ratio largely affected black and brown people. The myth led to erroneous stereotyping, causing millions of people of color to be locked up.

Experts warned that crack would lead to a lost generation of crack babies, their numerous maladies burdening society. Well, as we all know now that was untrue. The only sickness that came from that time was mass incarceration created from the minds of people that were supposed to be leading us into a greater future.

But the experts were right about the "Crack Era" leading to a lost generation of babies, the unborn babies of the prisoners locked up for more than two decades as a result of the Drug War. Young men that had the potential of producing children – that God-given right stolen from them because of a lie.

The 1994 Crime Bill that Chairman Biden oversaw, included children being tried as adults, and the application of the death penalty for sixty or more crimes. Talking about playing God, this bill that he voted for exacerbated mandatory minimum sentencing, causing even more mass incarceration.

Prison construction grants were ensured to states that changed their sentencing policy. A person convicted in states that cherished federal funding for whatever program they were launching made sure those convicted in their state, served 85% of their sentence.

Politicians that supported the Crime Bill will claim it helped reduce crime, but experts now say reduction can be contributed to things like an aging population and decreased alcohol consumption, nothing to do with more police on the streets or the government's "lock 'em up and leave them" policy.

Do I think Biden's apology was sincere? Hell no! He's fibbed too many times.

But I have conceded that he definitely did a better job than President Trump. Trump issued a non-apology to kids he lobbied to be killed for the Central Park rape. DNA would prove their innocence after seven years of their young teenage, years were wasted.

America needs fresh faces and new voices to lead us into the next generation, not the same ole tough-on-crime policies, and the upholding of Draconian laws that should have been long since deleted from the annals of legislation. We need sensible laws that doesn't target any minority group of people for the sake of an image to prove government is working.

A look at Portugal's drug policies will illustrate that after the country decriminalized the consumption of all drugs, drug-induced deaths plummeted. Yet England's prisoners can't seem to get this figured out. Yes, with America initially being England's prison colony, her prisoners, became the founders of the United States. The criminals of America overthrew her majesty, the queen, and set up a government modeled after the great Roman empire.

Socrates' voice was mighty as the Father of Western Philosophy in the Greco-Roman society. He believed that the best form of government was neither a tyranny nor a democracy, but instead government worked best when ruled by individuals who had the greatest ability, knowledge and virtue, and possessed a complete understanding of themselves.

I think even some politicians will agree (those with a conscious anyway) when it comes to how the government has handle America's drug policies, the brightest ideas haven't prevailed. Especially, how they have mishandled marijuana offenses. Any person still serving a life sentence or any sentence for what has been determined essentially a medicine, can't be considered anything but senseless.

And drug users occupying a prison bed is a complete waste of tax payer's dollars. These people should be in a treatment program.

Decriminalize all drugs and tax them, the problem disappears. Sell it across the counter, the black market would cease to exist, making it impossible for street dealers to keep pace with franchised priced drugs. Imagine a street vendor trying to sell prescription drugs, his sells would be terrible with a CVS Pharmacy on every block. And the crimes associated with deaths over things like market share would end. Employees of CVS aren't killing each other over market share.

U.S. still has the highest incarceration rate of any country, civilized or third world, 2.3 million people in jail or prison. Are we still a prison colony?

Multi-generational impact of the absence of two million people, will be detrimental to the families and communities they're from. Statistics show how the people arrested in the 80's and 90's that served over twenty years, affected marginalized communities. As these prisoners eventually get released, only punished for decades and not provided job skills, how will they get hired to have money for adequate food and shelter?

Prisons need programs to teach the incarcerated person a bankable skill. Instead of rotting away, years passing with no progress, the right program could help this individual to become productive citizens.

We need black politicians that will refuse to sell their people out for a donut. Kamala Harris, San Francisco district attorney, California state attorney general and first black U.S. Senator, now the first woman and the first black Vice President, congratulations! But when her history as a prosecutor is examined, it's marred in the same type of unnecessary tough on crime stances as the one the federal government enforces. In the 27 years of her enforcing laws in California, African-American incarceration rate went up to five times their share of California's population. Her state was one of the most aggressive in locking up young black and brown men.

Although, she didn't craft the bills or vote to have them enacted, she enforced unjust laws that incarcerated numerous black and brown men when she had the power to do otherwise.

Let's shed this lock 'em up mind-set. We have the advantage of over thirty years of research. Just as fast as the "Crack Bill" of 1986 was voted into legislation, we need to roll back all drug policies at that same speed. The prohibition on marijuana should end and marijuana should be legislated into federal law immediately.

Politics of the past doesn't speak of a greater day, but more of the same fallacy that waste taxpayer's dollars. We must take a comprehensive look at prison over-crowdedness by first looking to see what can be done about impoverished, marginalized neighborhoods. Why should any citizen of this great nation not be included?

When history records the devastation caused by the Crack Era, it will write that America was the most ignorant of any civilized society, the world's greatest super power weakening her own strength by locking up millions of her young men for decades, a generation of unborn children lost. Killing her own future soldiers, future employees, future leaders.

The historian will write that America went through a period of the most backward thinking, revisiting the Jim Crow era on the dark races. She incarcerated them to work in prison slave factories as Willie Lynch had advised her on the banks of the James River in Virginia in 1712, not only did he teach her how to control blacks by pitting them against each other over differences like height, weight, skin color, but the most instructive part of his speech was, "prisons will become the new plantations."

Yes, with this genocidal process, America forfeited her future? But she can be saved. When she stop electing politicians that are ruling as if they are the last generation to live on this planet, her policies will change.

How can America maintain her dominance with seventy, year old, well after their retirement age, navigating us with backward doctrines? Does a 70-year-old person even care about the future, is he or she even aware that people will still live in the United States well after they're gone. What motivates them?

Where will we be as a country in 50 years? Does these guys even have a long, term plan for the continuance of the nation. Does it include all of her people, unified under one flag, or will they keep us on the brink of a Civil War.

America has already mortgaged her future enough with a failed Drug War. It's time to repair the breach, build up the old waste places, make America smart again, make America a country that includes all of her citizens instead of going to war with some of her citizens. Even though our land seems safe from foreign invasion, it won't be, if we continue to divide our loyalties.

All the ideologies, no matter how slanted the next group perceive it to be, if it's born on American soil, it is still American. It's a known fact that we won't agree on every topic. What country does? But we should find a way to unite instead of divide! Unite under the fact that none of us wish to be a citizen of another type of government.

If a foreign power ever felt we were weak enough to be overtaken they would attack, that's what country's do that have a thirst for dominance, they seek power, world dominance. And if attacked by a foreign government, your Q Anon flag or BLM flag isn't going to prevent them from killing, torturing or imprisoning you. You are an American, no matter your differences, and your allegiance to a separate ideology, even an un-American ideology, will not save you against a foreign enemy. Whatever that ideology is, it's still essentially American and a foreign power won't care if you hate another race of Americans or not, they hate us all equally. The only way to maintain our standing in the world is for all of us to unite as Americans.

Now that Joe Biden is President and Kamala Harris is Vice President they have a chance to revisit lies they both have championed, and shape them into a truth that will lead all Americans into a greater tomorrow. Will they advocate for change, or will their arrogance prevail, refusing to reserve policies they authored or agreed with.

Citizens must also do their part. We must band together and stand up as one to demand that politicians work for us and not the opposite. We must refuse to continue living our lives as prisoners in our own homeland.

Standing together, is the only way that we will again become the Republic as the forefathers envisioned, a nation that serves all of her people. We must reverse JFK's philosophy, "Ask not what your country can do for you, but what you can do for your country," to the right philosophy, "for the people by the people." What can all of us do for each other to grow and prosper together? What can we do to become a nation that is all inclusive, every citizen feeling at home in America?

More than half the country hated President Trump because of his politics of chaos and the devastation his racist's doctrines wrought on our country. But I truly thank Donald J. Trump for his service. Firstly, because he released my uncle, Michael Ray Harris, aka, Harry O, after being in prison for thirty-three years. And secondly for giving us all a good look at what happens when America elects a leader that doesn't understand how to lead the whole nation. A leader that supports racist groups like Q Anon, Proud Boys and the KKK and other racist organizations.

Trump gave racist groups a voice, and helped them promote their twisted ideology, a traitorous manifesto that's out in the open now. These people actually had enough gall to lay siege on Capitol Hill. What drug were they on? These people would still be cloaked and shrouded as loyal citizens, some even hiding in plain view if Trump hadn't exposed them.

The audacity to storm Capitol Hill. Although their coup failed, the attempt was carried out. And now how many other groups or enemies will plot something similar.

We have all heard of the KKK, often called night riders, and the ignorant disposition they walked all day in. Their arrogance, fueled by this ignorance, would drag of a black man from his home in the presence of his children to hang him in the front yard. This definitely epitomizes the inferiority of their state of mind.

Racists police in those days, even unleashed attack dogs on innocent people, including women and children, and assassinated black leaders. Racist police was the majority of the force. Go against the establishment and find yourself face down in a ditch, dead. Do you want to revisit the horror of those times?

Both Biden and Trump's ideologies were shaped during the Jim Crow era, which I have coined, "The Age of Ignorance." As it is the case for any seventy something white person in this country. Is anyone under the illusion that men and women born during that era and didn't participate was complicit with their non-action, allowing the pressure of the times to dictate their response to the awful plight of black and brown people. Even the so-called good white people stood by and watched this torture. Otherwise, it wouldn't have been so widespread, and that mindset would have quickly ceased to exist, the perpetrators of such senseless acts would have either been in a prison cell or dead.

Even if Biden and Harris are no longer in office when you read this, we should let these words serve as a reminder to do everything within our power to prevent the atrocities of the past to ever happen again.

Silence is complicity.